BEAR MARKET

The smart guide for beginners with current strategies, of the stock trade life for the bear and bull market, and how to trade to trigger financial freedom.

LUDWIG VON MILES

LUDWIG VON MILES
© Copyright 2020 by Ludwig von Miles.
All rights reserved.

This document is geared towards providing exact and reliable information with regards to the topic and issue covered. The publication is sold with the idea that the publisher is not required to render accounting, officially permitted, or otherwise, qualified services. If advice is necessary, legal or professional, a practiced individual in the profession should be ordered.

From a Declaration of Principles which was accepted and approved equally by a Committee of the American Bar Association and a Committee of Publishers and Associations.

In no way is it legal to reproduce, duplicate, or transmit any part of this document in either electronic means or in printed format. Recording of this publication is strictly prohibited and any storage of this document is not allowed unless with written permission from the publisher. All rights reserved.

The information provided herein is stated to be truthful and consistent, in that any liability, in terms of inattention or otherwise, by any usage or abuse of any policies, processes, or directions contained within is the solitary and utter responsibility of the recipient reader. Under no circumstances will any legal responsibility or blame be held against the publisher for any reparation, damages, or monetary loss due to the information herein, either directly or indirectly.

Respective authors own all copyrights not held by the publisher.

The information herein is offered for informational purposes solely, and is universal as so. The presentation of the information is without contract or any type of guarantee assurance.

The trademarks that are used are without any consent, and the publication of the trademark is without permission or backing by the trademark owner. All trademarks and brands within this book are for clarifying purposes only and are the owned by the owners themselves, not affiliated with this document.

TABLE OF CONTENTS

INTRODUCTION 1

CHAPTER ONE 3
What is the Bear and Stock Markets?

CHAPTETER TWO 28
Bear Market Survival

CHAPTER THREE 48
Stock Market Investing - Navigating the Bull and Bear Trade

CHAPTER FOUR 67
Purchasing Guide into Bear Market Profits

CHAPTER FIVE 93
Financial Freedom for A Stock Trader

INTRODUCTION

A keep is the investor that presumes a specific business or perhaps a wider marketplace is moving past and might want to profit from the drop in stock rates. Collars are often dismal in regards to their condition of the business or inherent atmosphere. As an instance, whenever an investor is capitalizing over the Standard & Poor's (S&P) five hundred, then the investor could anticipate shares to fall and want to gain from the drop on the overall marketplace indicator.

Recognizing Bears experiencing ought to be expanded to any or all types of niches, for example commodity markets, cash markets along with also the bond industry. Even the stock exchange is at endless chaos as their bullish allies, bulls, try to get control. For your previous 100 decades roughly, the U.S. currency markets has increased by a mean of 10 percent annually. It follows that any long-term keep in the marketplace has missing dollars. Nevertheless, many traders have been bearish in some specific niches or possessions and bullish others. It really is uncommon for anybody to really be always a keep in every situation and at every niches.

Bear steps As they truly are wary in regards to the near future of this market, bears apply a wide selection of processes which, including traditional investment procedures, flourish once the purchase price decreases and hazard capital since it climbs. The growing of those procedures is called informative sale. This strategy could be actually the alternative of their traditional purchase-low-sell-high investment decision way of thinking. Short-sellers acquire low and sell high, however in reverse sequence, 1st sale after which purchasing as soon as -- the purchase price has dropped.

Short term marketing is potential by borrowing shares from the broker to promote. Considering making the profits from this bargain, the brief seller additionally simplifies the number of stocks lent into this agent. Its own goal, alternatively, will be always to replenish it in a subsequent time and in a lower price tag, permitting it to pocket the difference for good results. In contrast to trading, short sale is significantly more threatening. At a traditional investment, even as the collateral selling price can simply fall into zero, the client can simply shed the amount of money he's put in. With informative sale, the purchase price has the potential to increase to infinity. For that reason, there's not any limit into this worthiness that a brief dealer is predicted to get rid of.

Guide of the Bear quite a few highprofile shareholders are famous because of his or her strong attitude. Peter Schiff is among those creators understood in WallStreet circles whilst the most bizarre recall. Schiff, a stock broker and au thor of several investment novels, borrows unwavering pessimism on newspaper investments, like bonds, and even favors people of the inherent attention, such as for example minerals and gold. Schiff was commended because of his prescience in calling the Great Depression out of 2007 to 2009 because he pitched the U.S. market towards the Titanic at August 2006. This is supposed to be recalled, however, which Schiff has generated a few doom-and-gloom predictions in his livelihood who have not come to fruition.

CHAPTER ONE

What is the Bear and Stock Markets?

The Language bull and Keep Industry are Utilized to Make clear how fiscal markets do that is, if or not they love or depreciate. At an identical period, since the market has been driven with the behaviour of users, those words regularly signify the way users consider the company and the next routines.

In Other Words, that the Stock Exchange is a marketplace which Is to the increase. It's distinguished with way of a steady cost increase, such as inside the securities markets, even at the worth of these stocks of organizations. In such instances, traders consistently assume the up-trend should last at the lengthy run. Commonly, within this situation, the market of the nation is very good and also labor prices are very high quality.

Even the Stock Exchange, on the Flip Side, is One that's at downturn, commonly falling 20 percent or maybe more in the past peaks. Compare costs are gradually decreasing, leading to a downward trajectory that collectors hope will last, which then perpetuates the down spiral. The market is going to decelerate from the marketand unemployment may grow as employers start to put workers off.

Traits of this Bull and Bear Trade even though the industry state of the bull or keep will be indicated with the management of their stock exchange prices, you will find several corresponding features that traders ought to know of. Several of those facets are clarified from the next record.

Give and need for securities From the Bull economy, we find a popular and a very low offer of all securities. To put it differently, additional folks are still buy stocks while some can promote. Like a consequence, share rates increase as purchasers struggle available stockexchange.

Precisely the same goes from the market, when More traders are working to offer than to purchase. Generation is a bit more compact compared to distribution and, since a consequence, share prices are falling.

Invest or Psychology Considering that the behaviour of That the marketplace is determined and ordered with the way people translate the behaviour, invest or psychology and comment sway the method by which a stock increases or collapse. Stock-market buyer and success psychology count upon just one more. From the bull market, traders are eager to take part within the expectation of earning a gain.

From the tolerate customer, promote opinion Becomes bleak as traders keep to go their capital from stocks and to fixed income tools, expecting to get a constructive shift in the stock exchange. In summary, the collapse of funding exchange worth exceeds consumer confidence, which motivates purchasers to carry their own capital from their current market -- that, of consequence, causes an overall cost fall as out flows rise.

Alter in economical action Since the Businesses whose stocks have been trading online trades are a part of the bigger market, the stock exchange and the market will be tightly correlated.

The keep economy is interchangeable using a bad Market, due to the fact nearly all firms aren't able to create huge earnings because clients tend not to invest not quite ample. For instance, that reduction in earnings influences the style where shares are costed by people.

Throughout the Stock Exchange, the inverse would be Authentic, mainly because buyers have a lot more cash to take a position and have the ability to invest, which, throughout flip, stimulates and boosts the market.

Gauging Current Market Shifts the Principal determinant Of if the current market is bull or endure isn't merely the marketplace's Travels reaction to one scenario, however, how that it works within the very long run. Small changes are a temporary occurrence or even perhaps a change of this marketplace. It has really a lengthier duration of time that'll decide just how you understand industry such as a bull or a bear.

But not all of long cycles at the Market could be clarified as bulls or bears. Many times a company can proceed via a cycle of inflation since it locates advice. Inside this circumstance, a succession of downward and upward fluctuations will effortlessly balance profits and losses leading to a currency trading blueprint.

The Way Todo using almost any marketplace throughout the bull Economy, the optimal/optimally thing to get a investor to complete is always to make the most of growing charges by paying for stocks ancient, when you can do so, and just purchase them as soon as they've reach their stature.

Throughout the bull market, some reductions will probably be Modest and non permanent; yet an investor will normally invest vigorously and professionally in greater equity using a increased likelihood of producing a gain.

From the market, However, that the Probability of compensation is much larger as shares are regularly losing worth and also the ending is still not insight. Of course in the event that you intend to pay at the anticipation of the revival, then you're required to undergo a hazard in front of a rally occurs. Like a consequence, considerably validity might be understood in short-selling or more powerful investments like fixedincome securities.

An investor May Also switch into defensive Stocks, the outcome which will be influenced by expanding market requirements and so are resilient in the financial downturn and flourish cycles. You'll find organizations as products and services, that can be mostly possessed by the us government and invite men and women to pay for no matter of economical conditions.

The Truth Is That You Can Gain from accepting a Informative standing in the stock exchange, profiting from falling price ranges. Additionally, there are an assortment of means todo so, which includes small sale, paying for reverse ETFs, or even buying set alternatives.

The two bear and the bull's markets will Possess a noticeable impact in your economies, also it is really a wise concept to devote time to check exactly what the market does prior to earning a investment choice. Be aware the funding market place has ever needed a fantastic yield while in the lengthy term.

As the tidal pull controllers the occasions On Earth Earth, and also at the lack of this will reap fall and less aside, additional forces are always acting and reacting to eachother so as to produce the occasions of this talk industry. The language bull and keep market can easily be recorded, nevertheless they're quite hard to grasp. They really are the principal keys of this Trade, no one will tell specifically what ability will rule in exactly what time and to a long time. Much like usually the person that confidently forecasts the current weather just to then see its inadequacies, all these conducts are not easy to constitution. The moment they property, one particular witnesses their outcome, celebrates their wages, or induces compromises, as can be true.

This Isn't a Issue for an Informal Invest or. The associates of the business and your daytime dealer observed those incidents and faced with the consequences. The driving causes of those designs would be the sellers and buyers that are hence signed. This definition will be awarded into the trade as an entire, however to distinct securities or sectors.

Envision a Circumstance in which, to get your maximum Well-known motives, a invest or unexpectedly develops convinced and proceeds to purchase. Now visualize a circumstance similar to that having tens of thousands of clients that are swarming on stocks and purchasing in hopes of obtaining capital profits. This isn't just a fairy story, events of the type took place ever sold, and also the greatest stripes are seen from the nineteen nineties. Even the usa as well as other international markets have undergone a remarkable growth in the foundation of investment and commerce. Unprecedented situation have now prevailed.

The Social Gathering

The premises of all those opposite are Erroneous. The match has stayed interesting, and also the user has ever been imagining as . The close reliable quote, that provides credence to earlier averages, is the fact that the bicycle continues somewhere around 4 decades, the prior takes the increased section of this bull-bear cycle, even three decades, and also the latter will be satisfied together with 1-year.

The Actual testing instances to your buyer Are keep markets. Survival intuition and collapse prospects blur that the investor's opinion, and also yet one devotes problems and blunders through the duration of that moment; point. The speedy rate of talk prices in that time would be your protect of sensible profit-seekers. The discussion of aggression, aggression and panic would be your most unexpected progress that a investor could choose. Under those phrases, some thing goes wrong and also your afternoon that the trading dealer confronts a succession of losses. The consumer will be frustrated in regards to the idea of pacing. This kind of individual can't choose the most suitable choice, and the older warhorses of this Trade have fought to locate balance.

Virtually every grownup using a secure occupation will be Worried about cash; should they create a portion of it, then invest it, and utilize the things that they will have abandoned at a smart method. Try as possible, it is typically difficult to get a normal practitioner to store huge amounts of income on the rainy afternoon, as each single time you change, there is still another charge or investment demanding that your own money. As you've got to conserve a whole lot of cash to earn CDs or high-yield cost savings account really worth your own time, it is very likely that you have observed that the currency markets for a destination for a enlarge your personal savings. Once you are referring to buying in the very first time, then it is vital to receive knowledgeable about all the stock investigation basic principle.

You may consider investing only requires you To flip some money to your proficient agent or trader, then you may settle back and await the benefits to roster up in. Even though this can be a particularly time-management direction variety, it is very important to find it out may possibly also function as absolutely the absolute most tough. Whenever you could be receptive to become a lot more involved on your portfolio, then believing in regards to the industry evaluation procedure is often rather informative.

You will find just two Key types of merchandise Investigation, a fundamental investigation and also a technical investigation. Fundamental investigation is still the main method of longterm and more advantage shareholders. That's because those types of traders want to know more about asset evaluation and so are concerned about subjective considerations which can theoretically alter the ability of the stocks to earn dollars. Fundamental traders devote a lot of the time analyzing the organization's previous, fiscal equilibrium and promote desire to your provider's services or goods before buying. Work might be quite time intensive, however it truly is on average really worth spending lots of hard work.

The 2nd kind of inventory evaluation Commonly used nowadays is named technical investigation and also, unlike any fundamental investigation, this method is significantly more worried about currency markets volatility compared to business record or monetary operation. Professional pros conclude the requirement will immediately answer such as well as other basic things to consider without having further examine. Financial pros additionally conclude the economy continues to change from direction of tendencies and also these routines are all anticipated to reproduce by themselves. It's to the grounds of the assumptions the specialized analyst could simply rely on past economy fluctuations in a effort to predict potential stock behaviour. Many detail by detail traders utilize the elements of all kinds of investigation inside their own strategies.

Stock-market Growth & Bear Markets Fiscal market individuals are somewhat interested in business tendencies: equity markets and keep markets. We're frequently obsessed with all the most important subject of this monetary marketplace, also with good reason. After the bulls fly, the overwhelming most of these generate income in the stock exchange market; nevertheless from the tolerate economies that they lose their own shirts.

Trading Can Be a game from Which You Have to Master the blueprint so as to get to best outcomes. Your debt, the advantage or inventory exchange will probably possess many different evolutions that change perhaps not just daily, but in addition in about a minute for the second. It's critical to become connected with such improvements once they can be as a way to become capable of making the most effective and decisions that are successful.

The Idea of the bull marketplace may employ Into the style by which any product is demanded with clients. The saying can possess a humorous tone," nonetheless it is really a easy phrase in a exact straightforward world in which time is extremely rare. This was motivated by how the raging bull was so spectacular. He increases his ears in the atmosphere to check larger as well as dangerous to his competitor. About the flip side, it's frequently regarding the overall task of this current market, as most of investors within it may actually traveling naturally at an identical way for being a herd.

Even the Stock Exchange is quite a period in which the Overall blueprint in price ranges will be rising. This is sometimes pushed by means of an investor's assurance and elevated hopes or from economical increase. In such instances, most people normally assemble property investments, so cutting back the prospect of retaining each of their eggs into 1 basket. Wise buyers will be taking good advantage of those states to get paid major advantages.

You need to evaluate this notion into the Concept of this stockmarket to aid get . This monetary sentence can be a nod into how a keep slides his hands around the earth once assaulting. Because of this, it truly is predicted when the market is still downhill. In such instances, traders increasing their own expectations along with profits. They truly are constantly very wary about generating purchases that are new, and frequently they have a tendency to keep a way from industry until eventually they truly are somewhat more favorable.

As Opposed to the overall normal, when folks Are frightened to obtain some thing, that they don't have any reservations concerning getting a silver bullion. That's the reason why the amount of gold is climbing in situations of financial catastrophe. Being at fantastic requirement as most buyers shield their riches as products as opposed to as money, as they are sometimes marketed at greater charges.

Many analysts possess powerful technological Skills, but we maintain it uncomplicated. The overriding topic of the stock exchange is bullish (favorable, soaring) as inventory prices commonly grow. When shares have been up 20 percent or even more out of the prior non, the requirement for bulls is already born. In case the purchase price cycle increases and also equity price ranges on average fall by 20 percent or even longer, keep markets start off. You compute these inventory routines by monitoring a huge small business standard such as for example the Dow Jones Industrial Average or even the S&P five hundred Benchmark.

As soon as you are going to stay actively engaged with Bull markets to quit attempting to sell down markets, simply a little buyer will probably create Money in shares to retire . Moving back into the 1920's, you could really Maintain stocks at good occasions and more difficult, and also you'd have left 10 percent per year at the Long-term. To Put It simply, the Customarily Bull-market has continued more compared to Bear industry. To Put It Differently, securities have generally increased in value time.

Even the Stock Exchange Hasn't Been easy for Potential Buyers Since the entire calendar year 2000. The Most

Important tendency has spanned several occasions, and also just two tolerate Markets have defeated shareholders. The Very First decade of this new millennium was a "lost decade" as shareholders dropped funds for its Very First Time in person History throughout the period. That Is a whole lot to be hunted Herein Contrast to this important progress from the

Capital industry. Up Coming, keep markets will be An average of shorter long, nevertheless they maybe catastrophic. Secondly, large beats will require many years to recoup. Let us have a look in the recent history.

Approximately 60% of this marketplace fell in Only per year 5 was at first of March 2009. The most important tendency afterward shifted, also from March 2010 that the bull industry was enlarged its own stocks with greater than sixty percent commission. Exactly how can a $10,000 investment decision simply take place below those states: upwards 60% down 60%? The very first $10,000 will fall to $4,000, then that will definitely go up sixty per cent approximately $2400 to $6400. However you perform the mathematics, it is maybe not fairly, and you've not actually split upward or forced money .

It'd be wise to Observe that a 50 percentage Loss off set with way of a 50 percentage growth. As a way to interrupt after taking a fifty percentage reduction, you want that a completely growth to receive all around. Your $10,000 10,000 will fall to $5,000, then you'll have to move up a hundred percentage double for around $10,000. Bear markets are somewhat catastrophic, and also countless of collectors have thrown away their own money at the last ten years.

The Most Important Stock Exchange pattern generally Ranges in 1 calendar year to a number of decades. Pay attention into this business enterprise price in the event that you would like to create money from shares. In case the stock exchange increases excessive, market and require a while off the dining table. After the stock exchange disturbs traders to passing also sell them outside of despair, measure until the counter and keep obtaining. Avoid being duped should this appears an easy task todo. It really is hard to earn dollars from distribution from the 21stcentury. They had to express that this subject is just a pal of yours. The issue is the equity industry's key motif is shifting; however do not over stay your welcome at the bull markets and also don't throw away a towel at the keep markets in that elevation of this opportunity.

Neither dealer is Anticipating some Bear marketplace, nevertheless they're section of the business enterprise procedure. Therefore, if you should be likely to become always a longterm dealer from the stock exchange, it truly is much easier to look at just how exactly to live that the tolerate markets you are likely to manage in relation to trust you're able to prevent them. Below are some suggestions to secure you via a stock exchange cycle using small declines.

The Most Crucial Factor to Consider would be: Do not cave into this desire to market low understanding you're likely to lower your losses. More frequently than not, this ends in a durable loss as opposed to the usual fleeting loss in newspaper, since the bear market place additionally demonstrates. In the event that you actually require money, then it is normally advisable to depart from your shares independently and await the marketplace to recuperate.

Fairly, should you Have Enough Money, locate the Requirement for bears for always a purchasing prospect. In case the master plan is extended duration, then the bear market place might turn out to be always a fantastic moment to put money into stocks which can be feeble on account of the overall economy and maybe not as of terrible management clinics. Clearly, you are definitely going to wish to accomplish the job which means that you may know exactly the gap. The requirement for bears would be the Ideal time to present so

The Company enterprise Images decoding Sensex, currency trading & many of hardup states you will always detect the phrase'bear-market'. The inquiry now is"What is a Bear market place?'.

Bear marketplace is the State which each Company and stock broker worries, when stock-exchange reductions, past 20 per cent it truly is called being a'bear-market'. Whenever there is an alarming quantity of fall at the stock exchange prices, it's caused from the benefit drops of a company industry, or into this fall to some less costly expense in terror about the substitution influence. It is the exact contradiction of all Bull-market. Even the huge chain of traders sell their stocks off fearful of decrease earnings or by your lofty charges they've now. This leads to the cost to collapse in a sharp amount, resulting in a lot more traders to jointly use the specific same fear and also sell off their stocks far too; hence generating a enormous vicious ring.

By the 1970's There clearly was another Thing producing chaos within Beatles, it'd become the ongoing autumn of stocks that continued for a complete couple of years. The occasions like this scare off most of the traders and you'll discover a lot more uncommon chances of the fresh investor to speculate to the market. It truly is an apathy this awkward circumstance is the thing that maintains The bear-market managing, there is less or not as buyers in people that purchase the investments, even therefore that the selling-spree carries on.

The way the Bear- Economy Has an Effect on the investments-

Even a Bear-market Is Going to End out of your Price-fall of one's own securities. It can be an over night transition, even actually hitting you until you reach it. About the flip side, it can be sluggish, using almost monthly, at both predicaments that the finale the same; even the exact holdings of stocks will collapse into counts of money. The next fundamentals is going to undoubtedly be the fundamentals of those happenings.

Inch. Bear niches Are Normally bad just once You market your stock immediately or only wish your hard earned money at the present time.

2. When stock Prices fall and there is A existence of the diminishing tempo of economy investment, also this shows a wonderful property to get a longterm invest or.

The Most Important motto of this above Criteria will be to confirm the bear-market only demonstrates lethal to a finance if it's a concise term expenditure. If you ready to contain the shares for quite a lengthy period or more, it's certainly going to wind up staying truly a wonderful opportunity to buy in the present time. Even the"pros" you detect financing over web page counseling in your urges, which causes you to sell your stocks subsequent to purchase cost of your own stocks has diminished. The money leak on your pockets might have now been majority if you market it prior to the fall. Can produce a question to these simply your-self"If these certainly were those"pros" in stock markets, then and could not simply forecast the meltdown?"

What steps you choose in bear-market?

The Exact first action You need to consider Is always to seek out organizations which can conduct smoothly or persist for decades and a whole lot more. Even though we suggest a deep thought-work from this negative before investment, to obtain a good illustration if coca cola's stock price drops then remember that summertime will reunite back again. That brings us into the second rule.

3. Believe, behave and See the way to Distinguish the inventory expense from your corporation under-current, they don't truly combine over along shortterm trades.

In the Event You know to Observe the underlying Prospects of this downfalls, then you'll find the neglecting market-place as many fertile territory to sow your investments. You will always locate types of market-place coming into the previous better or grandeur. You will get paid profit even though some will hunt for this! Stock-prices of the businesses you had rough budgeting to get will more than likely be offered by significantly lower prices. They will rise back, you basically ought to hold back patiently and watch whether your heap of money rises larger. You had encounter stock-bearings reduce in contrast for their own retail selling price, which merely transports the conceptions of one's long-distance investments making healthy revenue.

When considering Acquiring stocks in their Low factors, it really is vital never to find egotistical and also confuse speculation having investment decision. A bear market place is not a fantastic moment to purchase insecure stocks thinking that you may decrease your losses having a sizable triumph when industry proves. In case the bear market continues longer than you count on it that a insecure inventory is much more inclined to drop substantially further or collapse altogether whether its company is from business for a result of insufficient money reserves.

A Far Better strategy Whilst purchasing stocks At a bear market place would be always to comprehend the corporations who've longterm operation histories and sufficient money reserves to journey out a lengthy wait market when the worst scenario scenario does occur. You're going to be much better off purchasing organizations that are fiscally powerful enough to defy a protracted economy contraction.

Additionally Hunt for Organizations that are Relatively recession evidence, like food, health, recycle and waste direction. Whatever the business is currently accomplishing, individuals carry on wish to swallow and also eradicate the waste. Medical maintenance is just a requisite rather than some luxurious. And re-cycling becomes an increase industry as purchaser optional spending declines.

You Might Have guessed Exactly what a bull Keep market is? The stock-exchange might be tricky as shares have been moving upward down and up. Subsequent to the business is moving down it truly is called a"bear market place". Subsequent to the marketplace is moving up it truly is called a"bull-market" Afterward if some particular inventory is executing well it truly is known as a bullish stock exchange.

S O key words Bull And Bear explain the Over all states of the stock market. They usually do not describe the short-term or daily changes. These states might make clear the condition of the market place more than a extended time frame, such as fourteen days. This does not suggest to mention the marketplace will go down or up throughout this age. It truly is additional to say the overall overall performance of this is referred to as Bull Or Bear in just a predetermined period frame.

Bull and communicates Perhaps Not Just clarify the Industry requirement they also signify the status of the marketplace. At a bull-market the current market is doing nicely. The inverse is valid inside a marketplace. Even the simple fact of these provisions is the total sign of the status of the certain blueprint round the stock market.

It is normally Known a lot of those Dollars is made over the course of a bull marketplace. This does not indicate to express that there is no dollars to become produced over the course of a bear industry. Possibilities lie inside of niches. The secret then will be to grasp their condition of drama therefore that you can execute transactions that may allow you to dollars. Afterall that's why folks swap around the stock market. When understanding that whilst the simple rationale for trading afterward it truly is crucial to receive understanding of the optimal/optimally way to implement a plan of investing in that might deliver a yield.

But, without a Shadow of uncertainty it is Consistently less difficult to make money onto the bull industry. When beginning you may possibly want to merely focus your consideration in order to increase your chances of making funds.

The Simple Fact of all Bear markets is moment Consuming. Getting back in at the perfect time when the fee reaches on underside. Afterward your only way is upward. You want to at all times be prepared for shortterm reductions. Trade logically perhaps not as emotionally. Be careful out there now and also perform your own assignments.

The movement of this inventory market, its Trends, whether or not down or up, are all understood because the"consciousness" of this market place. You'll find sure terms that are useful to signify market movements. A bear industry is distinguished by the downward movement of this market place above a period frame for being a bull economy is distinguished with a steady up tendency. In the same way, a inventory that is succeeding is termed bullish as a inventory with diminishing worth is called bearish.

Bull and keep references as applied over the Stock exchange regarding its entire prerequisites or"emotion" aren't properly used to signify short-term fluctuations over the market. A bear industry is typically a market where in fact the expenses of major shares have fallen in value by 20 per cent or even more over the absolute minimum duration of fourteen days. It ought to be claimed, though, a bear-market could observe a momentary growth in stock prices though they cannot be ongoing prior to the tide varies. To the flip side, a bull market place is indicated from the long-term and constant growth of key stock prices.

Traditionally, the Inventory Exchange has Represented the status of the nation's economy. Bull markets also have thrived whilst the economy had been acting welland unemployment has been reduced and interest levels were more not fair. Bear markets, even on the opposite side have commonly happened throughout examples in their economical downturn or recession. In such cases it's not uncommon for traders to expel faith on the market and organizations set about lay-offs a economic reductions. In serious cases that a bear economy can maximize an increasingly diminishing investor assurance owing to low worthiness of shares which might make a panic driven currency markets crash. Likewise a bull economy which is exaggerated might also be driven over excited investors and a current market"bubble" does occur. This"bubble" will burst and worth can diminish, frequently sharply.

When Most gains are created throughout bull Markets, opportunities of profits are all seen throughout bear markets. With an understanding of the characteristics of each and every sort of economy empowers traders to incur gains and profit in these trends. Of course, when the business is bullish traders tend to be somewhat more susceptible to get stocks upward. The surroundings will be favorable with market which's succeeding and men and women can have any surplus cash that they would really like to work with to"dabble" from the stock market. Under these conditions, the supply will be trimmed however, also the demand is elevated and also this also functions to drive fees high.

A keep marketplace, on the Flip Side, presents Decreasing inventory prices resulting investors to hunt to unload their stocks within an Bid to salvage what they're outside in these losses. Oftentimes, traders in some time Bearish economy will set their income into fixed yield instruments like trades Or mutual capital as they present much less of the hazard. As cash will be eliminated from your Stock exchange due of stock profits, the market exceeds the requirement along with The expenses of these stocks are pushed .

Evidently, the Simplest Period to Build Currency from the stock market is if it is bullish. When it is potential to have in at the beginning of upward trend, you find it possible to stand to benefit from the maximum from minding the most useful profits. The drops that happen through the duration of a bull-market are all momentary and in many cases are corrected quite fast. However, it truly is required to realize that the rising charges will steadily begin to fall together side the wise investor will soon discover just how exactly to"browse" the trends and be expecting that the market place peaks, and the ideal time and energy to sell before industry ends.

Bear markets do possess any fantastic Benefits though because they supply traders the occasion to buy stocks in buy prices. In spite of the bull economy where the secret to optimal gains is to enter in the beginning, the optimal/optimally chance of profit within an bearish marketplace is at the long run of the craze. Ordinarily, the values collapse, frequently much, previous to recovering that gifts that the purchaser using a optimal/optimally buy at a minimum cost. But, traders have to be prepared to possess a short-term decrease because charges dip previous to the upturn.

Shortselling Is a Well-known investment Program That happens throughout a bear industry. In informative sale, you promote inventory you do not possess in the anticipation of the more cost fall. This is sometimes accomplished in order if enough full time arrives to ship, you're able to buy the inventory for significantly less than you offered it. Compelling return investments for example as for example CAs and transactions may likewise be properly used to make income at a market. These"defensive shares" are more secure to acquire any given moment, regardless of the stock-exchange trends.

My consider regarding the Inventory Exchange changed a Week, because I have started to get and impulse a couple shares, some thing I haven't accomplished in a exact long moment. The current market remains inadequate and I truly do not locate any signs of an actual restoration nonetheless and undoubtedly not just a sustainable financial increase, nonetheless it appears the stock market is just planning to last increased anyway. Idon't need to fully grasp just why to build dollars. Now you make money in the marketplace by staying satisfied with all the market fad ahead of industry shows you incorrect. And it looks just like the overall intermediate-term fad is up.

Be-ing Right currently doesn't Make any difference.

The Stock-exchange Are inputting a confirmed Cyclical bull industry. That's an important element I'd like after I've already been contacting this a keep market place since oct 2007 and also by way of the prior couple months, but a week altered my own viewpoints. I'm going to explain the reason why in an instant.

First You Have to Understand That cyclical bull Markets are somewhat marginally different when compared with secular bull markets, even as they do not bring about most time highs, however certainly are substantial 8-24 thirty day period goes in a imperial trading stove, for example since you watched after a bottoms out of 1974 and 2002. After the bull-market completes the market-place averages subsequently go back to the imperial highs or input some kind of money trading scope.

Over All This Type of Market-place is tough to Investors in mutual resources over the lengthy run, simply because they end up retaining large reductions sporadically after which sit and make their losses once things turnaround only to reduce them. As the usual invest in and maintain indefinitely individual simply matches his wheel dollars is established possibly trading exactly the averages simply by paying for stocks out there averages as opposed to trying to get the market place for a complete lot.

I Would Not Have Any Clue just how Lengthy the bull Market will last how big the marketplace will go out from this here.

Everything I really do know is It provides an Possiblity to finally make an outstanding deal of profit private stocks in a simpler manner than individuals experienced throughout the past year 5 and also do not be concerned if you should be long you haven't overlooked anything, even as the bucks must be manufactured is just maybe not at all chasing the marketplace averages much larger, nevertheless in person stocks should they lineup to really go up.

There is just 1 S&P Five Hundred to buy, Inch DOW, also another NASDAQ, therefore partaking within the big event you would love to find the ETF's it truly is an easy task to"miss" But together with individuals stocks you'll find absolutely 1000s of men and women to pick from and additionally the danger to advantage will be way better inside these. Together with ETF's to develop significant dollars you ought to really go on gross profit ergo the incidence with the ultra-ETF's, however together with human stocks there is desire to limit to make a wonderful return, as you buy the perfect ones it truly is easy to create massive profits inside them.

In Fact you notice it circulates all of the moment; point. As an example just one stock that I bought per week reverted above 14 percentage on Friday by yourself. I'm convinced that you just may possess a inventory that you don't need you like you've purchased. You shouldn't worry with human stocks and overlooking, because there is another person round the corner. In no way pursue whatever.

Let Us Take a Look in the Stock Economy and What has compelled me to improve my own view of this.

In the conclusion of 2007 that I Started to figure out Each these signs we ended up likely within a market. Afterward in December 2007 I said the bear-market was supported from your a hundred and fifty along with 200-day moving-averages.

In keep markets All these shifting averages. Act as resistance as well as in bull markets they act as services. However, if the moving-averages summit and commence to return combined with market place remains underneath them for more than 6 weeks afterward you certainly are at a confirmed remain sector. Actually that's obviously my DEFINITION of the keep marketplace - perhaps not a fixed percent which the stock-exchange has to yield, however, also the overall price actions of the forex current market, that your moving-averages create completely evident.

You May flip this Approximately too although - As soon as the going averages are still acting as resistance and Begin to sew and also the market proceeds on it stays over it to get over six weeks afterward you are commencing a bull economy throughout the proceeding Typical will probably end upward service.

This really Is Just What we have observed happen in The prior fourteen days. From the March decision I felt the economy was over sold and we'd been going to be given a keep market rally that'll ultimately churns direct and out into New highs. As you would really love to stay adapting together using the huge tendency to bring in dollars and I considered down I experimented with brief a few times merely for ceased outside. In addition, I'd no concern with being erroneous regarding the market while in the feeling of "lost" onto a rally, even since I have know in a bull-market that the substantial currency is produced of other businesses and shares instead of industry averages.

In Reference into Them that which I saw from June Were lots of organizations that looked as though that they might have bottomed, but weren't just likely to proceed back into this coming month or two when that have been the case anyway. In case the marketplace proved genuinely bullish they would provide adequate entrance points then. That's exactly where we are now very.

From June Even Though Later getting ceased outside To the short side a few instances I begun to ponder if I was to the wrong aspect of things, however, none the less felt even if I'd been we'd still receive yourself a fantastic correction. The marketplace commenced June across the 200-day relocating ordinary. I said that in case it stayed over it to get two days then the activities will likely be affirmation that each one of the folks stating we are at a bull market place are still not correct. However, when it fell under it afterward proceeded into the 800-850 scope by ancient August then they would most probably be wrong after which we really should be prepared you'll finally locate the drops of March busted or evaluation contrary to your drop.

We obtained down you into The 870 spot around the S&P five hundred at the start of the calendar month also it looked whilst the correction might last far more time. However, the market-place maintained the service level and rallied upto earn a brand-new high past week. The potency of this rally last week will be what has shifted my viewpoints out of getting relegated into seeing that because of bull bull industry. Even the S&P five hundred was within its 200-day relocating ordinary now for two times.

For me personally that this Is in Fact a Truly Confirmation Moment whilst the purchase price actions in December of 2007 confirmed we're at a bear industry this price activity affirms that individuals're in certain type of bull industry. Yeah I'd not put in around the March very low, however virtually everybody who'd previously been participated in March ended up all through all past held and two all down the way in dread of"missing out on".

Straight back 2007 I pointed out Out how the Moving averages are saying we'd been in a confirmed keep market place to men and women and'd lots of an individual make angry and also offer me alist of explanations for why that couldn't be. Some stated that the Fed wouldn't enable the economy to collapse. They observed that they certainly were diminishing levels for example angry. Men and women on CNBC said that we were just in an short-correction. The marketplace did actually be more fine. I truly do not want to say titles, due to the fact this inch person compromises suits contrary to those that says any such thing crucial, however a famous identify might state that it's really a bull market place also in case you market you may miss on everything so an extraordinary offer of individuals had been only terrified death which if they marketed they would get left behind on gains.

Nevertheless, that the Market-place Task is that mattered then. And it's really all that things now. Iam not going to create exactly precisely the same error which the women and men who denied the the bear-market did . Who is aware of why it truly is increasing - it really is. It may be the the stock market is still considering that the coming bottom in actual estate charges each year out of now and can be moving up until several positive GDP quarters. It may just be the Fed is printing thus much money. Who is aware of, until the tendency has been completed it truly is precisely what the cause is. There is only additional money moving in to stocks in comparison to going outside there.

And you Additionally You might not Know it, however I Have desired to possess out there now in the marketplace for rather some time. I've been awaiting moving long-term different stocks, so as a fantastic bit far more cash might be manufactured from these enjoying with the ETF's - which has been my chief way for making profit the stock market because the bear market commenced - and also will be one I am currently left handed.

Provided The Marketplace Is in a cyclical Bull marketplace the bucks to become produced will be in respective businesses and stocks that are individual. We do not need to have the current market to move a complete great deal to bring in money within just them. It truly is tough to basically inform just how big industry will move up or to find long, however my guess is we can watch it go in to the very first quarter of 2010 and also we will readily see the S&P five hundred input the 1150-1250 after which. 1150 certainly are a 50 percent retracement of this high with the drop 2007 and all the March 2009 very low afterward that is aware of. By the 1970's the market-place traded all of up the way for its very own allowable highs after 1974 bear industry because of inflation. When we be given a great deal of inflation in a handful years out of something much the same in to the 1970's can be from the cards.

Or we can only Move up for yearly Out from this after which start out a brand-new watch industry in a dual dip recession because interestrates proceed up.

Facts Are That You Truly can not forecast Those kinds of stuff. Anything you Are Able to Do Is invest as Well as the overall Tendency of this market place and adapt as it is evident the typical Trend has changed. You don't have to really have in or out precise shirts. Should you Have using that stand industry in December of 2007 you would have stored a distinguished deal of Dollars. And also the Specific Exact Same goes, however I didn't move drawn-out in March At a ground by adapting from that which the market place is currently stating - and - that's creating Evident to people could earn a good offer of dollars to your future year with Moving long before stocks poised to out perform the stock market. Lots of Those Are definitely going to seem large.

CHAPTETER TWO

Bear Market Survival

Historically That the Bull-bear cycle Continues Somewhere around 4 years ago with most of the current bull-market continuing for somewhere around 36 months where as the Bear percent continues for nearly 12 months. Stocks also have trended increased through the stockmarket's history thus the possibility are together with you should you trade very long in comparison to short-term. These characters prefer currently being long most of enough sitting and time out several market intervals that are not an ideal necessities if you are permanent. Individuals than great states also offer you still another likelihood besides becoming money to get quick the business and try to profit from falling inventory prices. Attempting to sell brief in just a bear market place is often fairly rewarding . however, it truly is really a much tougher highway than a bull industry. To night we'll talk the reason why that really is.

Many novice Dealers and Far More Seasoned dealers possess a problem residing keep markets. The large part of the moment, it truly is because they've a false awareness of protection while they merely believe profits will probably continue in a substantial reduction way too long since they only undo their plans to inverse. It isn't so simple men and women. Bear markets really are many tougher to swap than bull markets. This really is on account of the mental rollercoaster of jealousy and panic that frequently hastens when stocks come at downtrends. Trend following approaches are more challenging in downtrends simply on account of this abrupt bear-market events which may possibly be somewhat abusive sporadically. These spikes will most likely produce short skips that may cause significant losses for those that require new small spots at the wrong instant.

Bear markets create It Far More difficult To turn short term profits compared to standard bull markets. We will intentionally quick stocks bear markets nevertheless comprehend that throughout all those periods, it really is harder to reverse consistent profits therefore that it's not our favorite means to swap. We consider that it's much more vital that you find prepared for that bear industry and also the consequent bull phase which follows we can endure and profit while still anticipating better terms. Take care not to dismiss the need for intending to survive the following keep market therefore you're well prepared for still another bull industry.

1 reason suffer inventories are somewhat more Complicated to exchange would be since volume drops harshly during many levels of an broad bear economy recession. This induces liquidity complications along with dangerous gambling conditions. Spreads can enlarge and slippage gains for the two exits and entrances. Short term sale opportunities will probably vanish stocks to get shares to invest up in numerous broker businesses. The most effective shares to quick may possibly possess no shares accessible to borrow. This really will be particularly bothersome whilst the stock exchange you've needed to short profits to decline at a downward spiral and additionally you are unable to find in a position to profit out of this. Quantity frees upward because fund managers grow dollars allocations to satisfy redemption orders and

also wont put extra income to use out of various other in flows of income as a result of anxiety about stocks decreasing farther. & most newcomer traders closed up shop as a result of a deficiency of attention from your economies through the duration of people endure market durations.

Still another motive Trading bear Markets could be acutely tricky is due throughout those instances, authentic selling price declines usually occupy only a few of these time that the downtrend conditions exist. Much like human shares, the indices drop quicker when they rise and additionally the promoting panic periods are generally eloquent and complete rapid. The rest of the stage the market siphoned back and on low volume whilst wanting to fix. In addition, the standard bear-market doesn't wind in the huge quantity capitulation that the vast majority of most women and men think may come about. These capitulation sell-offs do come about in bull-market corrections but rarely end keep markets. Fairly, keep markets end little by little as investors start to collected places as being a market-place base types. Most different participants will get small fascination with stocks considering that the very long stressing period doesn't provoke them going in to the again.

Our strategy to trading a keep Industry is Going to become one of predominantly cash having a combination of informative promotion and executing several long spots throughout countertrend rallies. We are going to behave invisibly by way of significant keep market states unless of course the intra-day charts indicate opportunities. Rallies and marketplace winners do supply first-class shortterm payments for buying and selling profits. Inch thing which people'll have to complete is tighten our retaining time as the business natural environment will change drastically. We are going to try to expect where brief covering events will probably come about and endeavor to receive a long time until the short ignites erupt. We are going to utilize the quick vendor's panic to earn a revenue, and attempt to detect resistance levels where by pure reversals could come about. As of the time we can undo right back into the side for resumption of their downtrend.

Being a keep marketplace Evolves, Abide by the Every Day Charts for key turning things and also act at constantly. Wait for favorable risk/reward opportunities and steer clear of getting whipsawed in your normal swings of investor/trader's anxieties and dreams. After all we are on protection, we will be on the watch for build-up and renewed care whilst the industry is currently in the long healing means of forming a base. These highlighting phases supply you with exemplary longterm potential for everyone individuals who have accurate market time. But bear at heart that entry at these instances will require execution against market place sentiment. In other words otherwise, you are going to be acquiring when no body wants such a thing else to accomplish with stocks. That is consistently tough to accomplish however the potential reward should you time it accurately may be astronomical.

The best way to Achieve at a Bear Market Place Stock-market

During this Report Today I Would like to Speak of a Number of tips, hints, and tips that only about everyone may utilize to earn money at a bear down or market stock industry.

When It Regards Investing from the inventory Exchange you'll discover in essence two main conditions or predominant topics that you're likely to should take care of. The very first theme is a bull market place and also at a bull-market stocks have been rising over the plank at almost any small business. Actually a bull economy simply implies that normally that the stock market is perpetually rising.

Still another Most Important Predicament which You're likely To have to handle would be a keep market place and also at that a stand market place stocks have been decreasing round the plank and that is that which we are at now since recession that were only available in 2008 and has now become 2010.

Lots of traders get Terrified and operate away Through a stand, simply attempting to sell each of their shares, hunkering down, and awaiting to get your ache to really go out together side the market place to undo to bull's market mode. Regrettably, the moment an investor does this they miss the occasion to create huge amounts of income since quickly as the inventory drops enough it might grow to a fantastic steal.

Imagine in case a Favored stock utilized to Swap at $100 a talk plus you also purchased that a great deal of it. Now envision a store swooped in and also exactly the specific very same stock now trades for $50 per talk. In the event you experienced that the stock at $100, then you may now put it into halfprice! Why don't we get real, this stock has no where to go but upward; preferably.

There is just 1 thing that an investor Must be Mindful of if investing in a bear industry. I'm talking a bear market rally. A keep rally will be just as as the stock exchange market abruptly begins to leap into a market. The gist with this business is straightforward; it moves from bull to endure, from progress into downturn. That's the heart of capitalism also it's assumed to serve similar to this.

The Problem is," The inventory market may leap Up during a endure and fool folks in to thinking that the marketplace has ended and we have moved to some brand-new bull industry. In reality we've not proceeded to some bull market place, we have just undergone a rack in which the shares temporarily grow upon the board.

Investors Some-times pre-order purchase considerably Onto a stand rally thinking stocks really are just going to venture up only to detect a quick period then the shares have dropped down to their very first endure marketplace well worth, wiping out all of the proceeds that invest or might've just received all through the rally. Thus maintain a watch out to keep rallies. It's extremely best to buy inside the launching of the endure rally and also market following the stocks have enjoyed price but before they collapse straight again down again.

Therefore that you have several very simple hints Which everyone may utilize to create money at a market.

Any person who has Invested their cash The stock market for substantial periods of time, understands their trades will soon move down and up in price. This does occur not just daily but hourly and at times second by moment. There aren't any guarantees, either inch manner or the other.

The Certainty of Transform

These significant Swings in worth happen with Ostensibly noise not. The share costs of this finest, high grade bluechip businesses on earth can reunite "in closeness" with every thing, and keep on being if the exact advice with this time be inferior .

When modifications gleaned from Your inventory Market, it's usually called being a bull or bear industry. Even in "bull markets" over all costs transfer upwards, and also at "keep markets" charges yield. Topical, and also fully unrelated occasions can possess a profound influence on the managing of inventory prices. Economic stories, Federal Reserve encounters, industry earnings statements and data occasions all impact inventory markets.

The Expense with This Generally speaking stock market Is frequently quantified by their "indices". These are a representative basket of company stocks, such as the Dow Jones Industrial Average, comprising 30 Large companies, and also Additionally the S/P Five Hundred that is the best 500 largest Earnestly traded companies from the U.S.

Investment Decision and Feelings

Investors Can Readily Get trapped at the Excitement and frenzy of the roaring bull industry. In the utmost they examine their inventory costs every five full moments once positive opinions abound and begin counting their"paper gains" although imagining tropical holiday vacations.

Along with also their expects Become dashed if a surprising Negative change of occasions swings expenses in the other way, to some market. If a person appears at a historical stock-price chart, it isn't hard to observe that the regular - inventory prices typically return substantially quicker once they proceed up.

Essential Programs Around Bull and Bear Markets

Should You Obey These hints You're Going to Use strong investment fundamentals at play:

Purchase Excellent Investments

Make sure They've been fully assessed by Someone together having an critical practical experience to achieve that. This can be rocket sciencefiction. These are all exemptions that you should truly feel comfortable owning throughout thick and thin, unless of course a considerable variable particular into this firm has changed. The firms that regain their losses following bear market endings, would be the great businesses with sturdy fundamentals and procedures.

Maintain Sensible Expectations and Keep Tranquil.

Several New Traders Minimize their Tooth throughout The tech boom of the 1990's. They unexpectedly experienced the capability to buy and market stocks of the particular, by way of Internet-based brokerages. They're, yet, in essence blind to inventory investment decision most useful clinics.

Thus, their Expectations were large For its future. 1-5% - 20% earnings per-year grew to become the newest benchmark. Regrettably, these exact same shareholders watched enormous proportions of those portfolios vanish following the next crash.

The Stock-exchange Has shrunk approximately 7 Percent yearly returns within the very long term. Year annually Yields, on the Opposite hand, Are constantly unsure and unknowable.

Know Your Risk Tolerance

When Charges Decrease and You Wind Upward Beginning to fear, know you've taken on an excessive amount of threat. Prosperous merchants seem that the"keep markets" at an occasion when shares are"obtainable". They know that their favorite businesses indoors and out, therefore they truly are certain and don't fear. At case the specific situation worth, they still get greater stock.

Just inquire Exactly how Much It Is Possible to Afford to risk whilst still maintaining your own objectives. If you're looking for that future, you're getting to base your investment decisions on both fundamentals and fundamentals.

Basics comprise Possibility diversification and Your life situation. Basics simply take under account Assessing volatility and metrics yields. They aid ascertain how"affordable" or"high priced" an inventory is. High priced stocks drop quickly and tricky in a market. Lots of traders heard this lesson following the industry crash in 2000-2001.

It Is Crucial to Keep up adequate Bandwidth along with also a cash pillow. Life has been full of unexpected occasions like health crises. In the event that you advertise through the duration of tolerate market lows as you would inadequate income savings available, then you're sure to get rid of substantial amounts. Around the reverse side, in case you keep a more specific percentage in low, safer, more additional liquid investments, then and then you definitely are going to be more happy whenever you want to compose this evaluation.

Truth Is a Virtue

In General, the Best Strategy Is to remain Patient by way of bull markets and also be far competitive throughout bear markets. It's the opposite of what many typical shareholders do, but what exactly the planet's best investors are doing. Keep in mind, no matter how the experts have use of improved information and also their'sweetspot' decisionmaking capability has been discredited through years of instruction.

The Optimal/optimally Method to Get a Handle on Your Present Assets just in the event the economy crashes

In the Launch of the Industry accident, maintain Economy, or maybe an even temporary downturn, It is essential never to fear and stick to the herd. Though the following down cost moves have undesireable impacts on portfolios, then the idea about that you are in threat will wholly depend upon your own goals like a trader or trader.

For starters there's not Consistently a necessity to fear a market-place Recession since you're thinking about that the long-term trajectory of this stock market. Bear markets usually do are much briefer compared to bull markets, which is the main reason the stock market has general -- rose in price tag. Byway of example, the ftse-100 can Drop-in price tag by not exactly 4000 details and also be in a increased amount as it'd been 20 years past, inspite of both tolerate economies between. But because we will undergo at one moment, the potential risks entailed in downturns will wholly require the direction that you utilize to pay inside these.

Many dealers who Desire to reevaluate the Impact of those shorter-term Sector Declines, can choose to promote their talk portfolio. But this tactic is dependent on risk-appetite and reachable financing, since it entails launching a few spots.

Do You Have to Learn more concerning Investing? Proceed into IG's share dealing services.

For traders, downturns and maintain markets Offer exceptional chances for profit Since derivative product will permit you to speculate on falling and rising markets. Using derivative goods, it's likely to initiate a location on securities without even the need to get the inherent advantage.

Bear-market investment: the best way you can Earn cash when costs fall

You Will Discover Quite a Few of Techniques the two Investors and traders can profit from current market downturns, or even at minimum, shield their holdings that are present out of losses that are unnecessary. These include:

- Shortselling
- Dealing short ETFs
- Trading Safe Haven resources
- Trading currencies
- Moving extended on penny shares
- Picking out high-yielding dividend Shares
- Trading options
- Paying for in the bottom
- Shortselling

Most Likely the Most Frequently Encountered System of Progressing every time market declines, is shortselling. There really are a lot of means a individual can Shortsell, according to what niche you'll really like to swap and also the merchandise which you want touse.

Main-stream Shortselling

The Traditional Procedure involves borrowing The discussion (or some various gain) in your broker and attempting to sell it directly at the marketplace cost. In case the economy comes with a continuing number of downward movement, then then you are in a position to buy the stocks straight back once again to have yourself a smaller price in another day. You would subsequently reunite the stocks into this lender and simply take house the difference at cost because profit.

However, should you're incorrect as well as also the marketplace started To grow -- significance the downturn has been just a retracement -- you might have to buy the stocks straight back into the greater selling price tag. It truly is well worth noting that which you Shortsell, there is the possibility of boundless reductions since the theory is that there is zero limitation regarding what much a marketplace can grow.

Shortselling with derivatives

Shortselling Is a Critical goal of Derivatives trading it self -- the merchandise are rigorously insecure and require their particular price tag from your inherent selling price tag. Derivatives don't demand the trader to really have the assets or stocks under consideration.

If you swap CFDs or disperse bet, You are going to have the option togo both long and short so it will be potential to gain from economies that fall at price tag, along with people that grow.

If you disperse Wager, you are placing a Bet regarding how a particular strength's cost has been led. If you begin a concise spread bet standing, your advantage will be dependent on the expense going down, then supplying you with the specific very same effect like a normal shortselling placement. Whenever you exchange CFDs, then you definitely are purchasing a deal to swap the exact gap between your launch and last price of the asset, within this example a stock exchange. You had start a position 'promote' that a CFD.

Can you have to practise shortselling? Open up an IG demo account to swap in a secure setting.

While We've largely been Concentrating on Downturns in securities markets, shortselling pertains to many different markets also, for example currencies and crypto currencies.

Dealing Short ETFs

A Concise exchange Traded finance (ETF), or even Reverse ETF, was forced to profit once the inherent normal declines. They truly are included of lots of derivative merchandise, largely futures .

It is Much like Shorting an security, Apart from As opposed to borrowing an benefit to market, then you are buying the market place. Thus, reverse ETFs enable investors to profit at a downward market, with no the need to market any such thing specific.

For Instance, If You expected the FTSE A hundred to de crease value, you'll put money into a concise ftse-100 ETF. In the event great britain grade did fall value, then the quick ETF will increase.

Inverse ETFs are Usually Maybe Not believed of Long-term investment vehicles, even whilst the trades they truly are predicated on will possibly be obtained and marketed daily from the finance supervisor, that means that there isn't any guarantee of its performance. Ratherthey are frequently employed by shareholders to advertise their conversation portfolio contrary to greater short period reductions.

Short term ETFs are considered a less insecure Alternative to antique shortselling, as the utmost decrease could be the sum you have put in from your ETF.

Know more about buying ETFs

For traders, Speculating on short ETFs Stays a viable direction of cashing in on current market downturns, as much the specific very same fashion because investors, as they only opt to'invest in' the market place. However, merchants might have a concise spot over a ordinary ETF. There isn't exactly the specific very same condition to rely on on inverse ETFs by yourself.

Discover More about Dealing ETFs

Buying and Selling Safe Haven tools

A Safehaven Benefit Can be a fiscal instrument That generally retains its well worth -- also boosts in price although the more wider economy declines. All these tools are all linked towards the current market, that means that they truly are many times employed by investors and traders to get refuge throughout industry declines.

In theory, you'd possess a Very Long position Onto a safe harbor, in order to find all set for economy downturns. It really is known as being a stand-in for finishing moving or positions brief, because it enables one to hedge any present holdings.

Normal cases of Safehaven resources Include golden, authorities bonds, government bonds, that the united states dollar, the Japanese yen and Swiss Franc. Nevertheless, it is essential for investors and traders equally to keep in your mind that because an advantage is recognized as a secure harbor, will not ensure it's going to be the in each and every business downturn.

When we select the exact Example of gold, then to place Money to the safehaven edge, you'd like to get the authentic rare alloy to get a shop of price. However, if you are merely trying to take a position concerning the worthiness of secure havens, then you need to utilize derivative goods in sequence you didn't need to simply take delivery of this advantage it self.

Learn More Regarding the Best Way to swap Safe haven resources

Buying and Selling Monies

You'll Discover Monies That Are usually Used as secure havens during intervals of monetary reduction, but this really is only inch approach to work with forex market for being a hedge from economy downturn.

A nationally Currency is Dependent on this Wellbeing of this national market place, that means any perceived reduction on the market in the high, will execute to the buy price tag of their currency. Once an market can be considered weaker in comparison to additional global markets, then its own currency will likely accrue comparison with other foreign currencies. Byway of example, throughout Brexit negotiations, the governmental chaos and doubt influenced the appeal of investing at the great britain. This detected volatility drama upon the FTSE 100 and British pound sterling.

Traders may have a Ranking over the Purchase cost of the decreasing economy by choosing for quick a currency. Whenever you swap money, you're essentially acquiring one currency and selling another. Byway of example, whenever you advertise GBP/USD, you would try it at the big event which you believe the worthiness of this pound will probably drop in relation to US buck.

Know about that which foreign exchange is and also how it works

Throughout market Downturns, most Industry Participants might take to to grasp the bond between market prices and stock price ranges therefore as to organize their own positions to get your volatility receive the absolute most from almost any decreasing price ranges. However, there isn't necessarily a relationship that is simple, which makes it crucial for traders to perform extensive investigation prior to beginning a stance.

Moving Prolonged on penny stocks.

Investors may Regularly Try to diversify Their portfolio with the addition of rules that are defensive. These really are the shares of organizations that are regarded as purchaser fundamentals, therefore that their services and products are all demanded no matter of the state of the marketplace. These could incorporate meals and beverage makers and usefulness organizations.

Once a market is performing well, Investment will flow to'cyclical shares', that are the firms that produce products that are governmental. Where as every time market is experiencing a time of reduction, the attention would go into companies which deliver customer prerequisites.

Find out 7 Defensive Shares Which can increase your own portfolio

Like secure havens, Traders possess a Inclination to start piling in to penny stocks if bearish ruling arises. Traders can additionally monitor defensive shares being a way of differentiating whenever the economy experiences a big change in mood, utilizing the businesses because of hint for your wellness of the broader securities industry.

Picking out High-yielding dividend Stocks

While Concentrating on Growing stocks is now The new benchmark, these broadly speaking have most in bearish niches. That's since if their investigation isn't copied with powerful fundamentals -- significance that they truly are over-valued -- which the shares may possibly have farther to collapse.

Looking for Dividend Shares could be quite a Excellent means to discover really worth among a declining economy. Though a firm's share-price may possibly simply take a winner, however it doesn't necessarily suggest the fundamentals of business are not useless. When your supplier is nonetheless developing a stable balance sheet, then they then can spend dividends.

Learn-about the Maximal yielding Money Stocks to watch at the great britain

It's Possible for you to use on-line Tools such as IG's inventory Screener to discover organizations having a tall price return. Once you have recognized a investment stock, then you also will either undergo our talk coping agency or agree to your company's share cost by opening a trading up accounts.

Buying and Selling alternatives

Trading Alternatives Savings gives one of with the Most useful, however maybe not the responsibility, to sell or purchase the underlying asset at a specific price with way of a established stage of buying. Alternate options are broadly useful for pure speculation, but however they truly are also a well-known way for traders to hedge from decreasing share prices.

You Will Discover a Range of Options Tactics which might be properly used, two typical kinds would be:

- Purchasing Established choices
- Creating covered calls
- Purchasing Collection Possibilities

Whenever You Get a Established Option in a inventory, You would try it from the viewpoint the supplier will fall value. Investing in a pair provides the best to market stocks in the attack expense -- hence in the event the inherent selling drops falls below the strike price tag, you could exercise your choice and promote the shares in a increased price tag.

By Method of Instance, let's mention shares of Company X Y Z are currently trading at 35, nevertheless, also thought these were likely to reduce worth. Now you obtain yourself a place option with a strike price of thirty to get a weeks' period. In the event the right time of expiry, the industry selling price was twenty five, then you could certainly do your put option and sell the shares in the greater expense of thirty.

The worth of the location Alternative Will Increase As the underlying marketplace declines. Oddly, its worth might collapse in case the inherent economy price becomes closer into the attack price tag.

Investing in a set Choice can be seen Less risky that shortselling the stock exchange, as although the market place could grow rise, it will be potential to just enable the possibility perish. Probably the maximum you are going to get rid of is that the top you have paid out to initiate the positioning.

Composing Coated Phone Calls

Composing a protected Telephone suggests that you Are promoting a call option contrary to an inventory that you possess -- ostensibly, you are taking that the obligation to market that stock towards the ruler of the telephone solution. In case the buyer chooses to exercising the possibility, you will have no option except to market your stock exchange. This normally means there's a limit regarding the entire sum of benefit you can create.

If a Current Market is Declining, you will be Contemplating attempting to sell your own stocks any way, so writing insured calls are sometimes a superior approach to get paid more cash outside of this buy price. The buyer will probably be hoping the business will probably rebound right back, therefore in the event the stock doesn't grow, it is rather probable that you'd be able to keep up your shares together with all the top quality.

No matter Whether the holder Exercises their phone choice, so you would certainly be paid a premium to carrying to the prospect of composing a call.

Paying for at the foundation

Subsequent to the stock Economy falls, the Worthiness of favorable and unwanted stocks alike can fall. About the flip side, the fantastic types will almost certainly recover. If you should be ready to recognize businesses that are powerful, then the Dropin costs will make up a fantastic purchasing prospect.

It is very important not to only dash to Choose the exact 1st inventory you see -- no thing its position beforehand of this marketplace. Most traders and investors may use fundamental and technical analysis to identify stocks with a great prognosis. You should at all times inspect the company's balance sheet, test and management program and personal debt levels.

Loan Providers will probably be looking at that companies will be Best set to pay for off their debts, and recover out of the bear-market -- ergo, by assessing just how credit-worthy a creditor believes a business to function as, investors can spot amazing chances to buy from the bottom. Bond evaluations of AAA, AA and also a indicate that a supplier is supposed to become creditworthy, but some thing beneath is considered a chance.

After the stock has Attained a Valuation that you think is sensible, you're able to aquire. It is Crucial to Remember the talk cost possibly wont bounce straight back fast however should You're convinced in your own search, you should become pretty much ensured it Will eventually.

CHAPTER THREE

Stock Market Investing - Navigating the Bull and Bear Trade

Stock Exchange Tendencies are Often Clarified With among two colloquial states: the Bull Market and the Bear industry. The market place changes backwards and forwards among both these market states.

A bear market is really a term which Displays the In general recession of this present market place, or diminishing stock prices. Around the reverse side, the bull market place is still only the opposite - that the positive growth of this market place's stock prices.

Individual shares together with increasing worth are Called stocks that were foreign, whilst folks experiencing a discount are called nominal shares.

Indicators of both Bear and Bull Shares

You May Not Correctly categorize the inventory Exchange tendency just about the lands of temporary details. Determinations of bull or bear markets expect that the overall trend of stock charges over a few of age.

To Take One Example,, There'll inevitably be Temporary ups in some stand marketplace and short term drawbacks in a bull industry. So the stock-exchange varies each evening, however, it really is crucial that you gauge its own longer-term overall trend.

Fiscal Indicators with This Business

The Stock-exchange Has a Tendency to signify the Complete condition of this current market, receiving a wide selection of similarities with all the entire industry.

An bull or bull Market could Acquire mild Rates of fascination and quite a minimal unemployment rate. Confidence from the stock market is high, and also the performance of stocks on ordinary slender or-so might be ardently constructive.

Some-times Wherever the Marketplace Is undergoing An financial recession, we detect elevated heights of unemployment and also a few of awful financial indexes. Inside this category of market, traders have a inclination to get rid of confidence from the present industry, and could market their stocks in enormous amounts.

EX-treme bear or Bull markets are not Wonderful For the inventory market, together with EX-treme producing a unique pair of anxieties. A huge market can hamper economic problems because traders dash to ditch their shares rapid to reduce their own losses.

Sturdy bull niches lead to A more"bubble" of stock wealth constructed like a consequence of both overconfidence of shareholders. Last but not least this bubble popsup inducing substantial issues into the overall performance of shares. If these kinds of bubbles burst, companies expire.

The Bull-market

Bull markets attract individuals that to desire to Buy shares. The performance of this marketplace and also the stock market will probably undoubtedly be shifting positively, helping to make it an wonderful time and energy to buy quite a few investors should they make investments premature.

Investors frequently need additional cash through The fiscal predicament of the bull industry. About the flip side, the increased desire and shortage of distribution for shares can cause the inventory price ranges to eventually develop into inflated, either or over valued.

It Might be easier To Earn a Profit out of A bull marketplace as the inclination of this current market is shifting upwards and everyone knows. But the current market and also the stock exchange market experience a second downturn within its cycle of ups and drawbacks.

For Traders, the Curiosity crucial comes from Accurately ascertaining the changeover period at which industry begins to collapse afterward require atleast a couple your profits by investing in part of one's stocks before to getting negatively influenced by this downturn.

The Bear-market

The keep marketplace could be Acutely difficult To browse, specially to get a rookie trader. Investors utilize quite a few one of a kind investment plans to try to generate the absolute best of the poor circumstance.

Certainly one of these Methods is called"brief Purchase," which can be actually the sale of stocks as you anticipate that its charge will last to reduce. Afterward your purchaser could get the shares straight back once again to find yourself a lot less expensive.

Other investors Elect to focus Only on investment in a great deal more stable stocks such as government possessed utility corporations since they truly are less insecure.

In case You are excited No thing what Happens from the investment decision market place or you're an investor, then you've got to happen to be alert to these provisions'maintain' and'bull' marketplace. Lots individuals attended across those states via the internet or about corporation platforms discussing financial niches. Recognizing that the difference in between a bull and bear industry could be a great process to comprehend these terminologies me an.

A keep economy Describes a stage in which a Industry is really on the decline which time can be broadly speaking linked to all the stock market. When shares experience a constant reduction within an extended time frame, the market place can possibly be clarified as diversification. This will happen past a number a few weeks or even longer. Just how can you spot a market? Evaluating how a sign does is just one effective way of comprehension perhaps the business is currently really on a reduction or never. By way of instance, S&P five hundred and DJIA could be utilized to examine decreasing markets. Once that the S&P five hundred has been significantly lower than 15% to get a complete calendar year, the European market place can possibly be clarified as an established industry.

About the Flip Side, A bull marketplace would be your Reverse of the bear industry. In scenarios in this way, market can possibly be clarified like being a bull market place when stock-exchange prices undergo a ongoing rise which is higher compared to normal regular. Exactly the exact same as in a stand market, indexes have been used spot a bull industry. For instance, in the event the normal return on an index is broadly speaking 1 2 percentage however for a reason that it continues to be at 16 percentage or more to a particular time, this really is considered being a bull industry.

Thus, the causes of a Bull or bear industry? It truly is well worth mentioning why these markets range depending up on the monetary operation. In case the current market is not succeeding or there exists a monetary recession, the economies reveal minimal characteristics and come back for a result of the terrible financial occasions. In the event the monetary occasions are shining and also the market place is succeeding, the consequent effect can be that a bull industry.

These Days many People see a Bull marketplace and Become tempted to speculate in the slightest. This is simply not a wise way as in certain instances, a few stock expenses in many cases are in their summit plus a few do not comprehend it. Whenever you buy a good offer of shares as soon as the expense are obtained, there is a possibility with the cost beginning to shed specially when you acquired them whenever they'd been at the summit price. But the expenses may possibly don't really go upward and therefore, you might perhaps not get any profits in the expenditure. Precisely the same notion applies to the keep market. Otherwise, you might choose to spend since inventory prices come at the floor and therefore you anticipate them to begin rising. However, there exists an opportunity that they can keep going .

The Ideal Time to Put Money into the inventory Exchange is whenever the marketplace does out and outside of downturn. It truly is broadly speaking as of that point when the niches begin to love plus it's difficult to foresee what is going that occurs within the not too distant future. For traders trying to sustain their own threats very low, it truly is crucial make sure consistent investment decision and also concentrate far more about investment in a bull-market and spend focus on purchasing a market as a result of higher uncertainty related to this.

A Bull-market along with also A Bear-market are deemed necessary Chief trends. A principal tendency could be that the status of the market place which is strong over the total market place and commonly continues for somewhere around per year or two more.

The Expression bull Market-place can be Utilized to refer To a up trend around the present industry, leading to investor assurance that might lead to rising worth of stocks. There exists a normally sizable volume paying for trend, together with shareholders expecting their shares to become more at the days ahead. Due to the fact large selections of traders ' are transferring together into purchasing trends, the set has been also called being a herd.

A bear economy May Be the opposite of the bull Market place. It's actually a downward tendency or maybe a falling economy. Investors usually are less likely to devote their cash and usually do not display acquiring pledge. In fact, they truly are more susceptible to promote their shares. A awesome example ever sold is the stock market crash of 1929, resulting from the truly amazing Depression. Although perhaps not all of bear markets will be the acute, actually, to become contemplated a bear market place, an expense decrease of 20 percentage on a short term period can be authorized.

People not active daily Investing or around the Trading ground can find themselves encouraging the tendencies, specially in a market, suggesting possible declines at a portfolio.

Most Women and Men know Of equally Fantastic animals we normally connect together to all the stock market. Most likely the most effective known are the bulls. These reflect investors who are pushed by greed and greed. Even the bulls can be found down Wall s-t when more times have been perceived ahead, flood industry making dollars to buy stocks and forcing costs high. Bull markets are all niches which rise pervasively within time we all adore bull markets - everyone makes income!

The bulls' Fully Guaranteed Enemy are the bears. Envision a maintain appearing from hibernation following having a cold wintermonths. Cranky and starving is not a fantastic combination. Envision currently putting this rack having a sharp rod and what he would do for your requirements personally. Well that's virtually what the bears perform to talk about costs at market! These markets have been caused by shareholders who have hardly any faith in the means of charges to rise and so desire to advertise. Driven increased by stress and pessimism the sparks crushes expenses .

There is just another less Wellknown Monster I have these days found explains many traders at this time. At every single completely free seminar I've inked recently I've been requesting attendees to participate in a questionnaire in the place where they declare on their own to eventually become bulls or bears. What's more, as the market place has unraveled, I am locating much less bulls, more sparks, however more of one other category - those who actually don't fit in to camp. When pushed the niche that they declare themselves as fence-sitters they don't really possess any clue at which the is transferring and so me an to'bury their head in the sand and then expect the very best'.

Thus my next group of monsters The markets - that the ostriches!

My Dealing coach Frequently explained the Inability of traders to do something in markets that are significant as the'ostrich process'. This calls for deferring behaving one way or the other from the anticipation that things will probably get improved, or only dismissing the specific situation altogether. The theory this is potentially'Everything you don't know can't harm you'.

Many adopt the Ostrich Method Out of'analysis paralysis'. Determined on the deluge of advice facing shareholders which they are puzzled and also lose the initiative to act. Fleetingly they wouldn't know the best way things to do should they really desired to. That really is infrequently the optimal/optimally alternate as niches may and frequently perform shed much further than most expect. Getting down half the manner stays greater compared to only holding each one the way in the floor. Most only assume yet, fairly wrongly, it is also late to act plus also they can likewise persist.

It isn't ever overly late to act. Very Excellent Investors are crucial. Much more importantly, exceptional investors really are crucial in Adhering to a plan. Ostriches about the Opposite hand are all indecisive and do not possess A plan.

As my mentor Might say"There Are excellent positive aspects in adopting that the ostrich process. At the least together with your mind in the sand you are unable to find out what's occuring. This is reassuring to get a few however there's also an important draw back way too. Together with your mind in the sand it normally suggests that added fragile portions of one's own body are somewhat susceptible. And that's maybe not perfect for everyone!"

Stock analysis Is a Critical element S O As to blatantly produce inventory exchange predictions. In reference to particular finance in addition to that the accretion of fiscal wealth, a great deal of women and men appear towards the stock market. The most important rationale is simple: Participating from the stock-exchange is now stimulating. But just as with any kind of investment, then you will find always challenges and dangers entailed. In order have the ability to engage in it safely, you want to equip your self together with applicable advice and also formulate strategies which operate and also maintain you comparatively safe and sound. That really is essential because there is no fool-proof approach regarding stock deciding. The perfect system for just one to survive this particular rollercoaster about this project is to maintain your self informed and also to stay authentic to predicated plans for staying afloat.

Stock analysis includes two Distinct forms: Technical and essential. Both these are excessively significant elements in establishing the management of this stock market. Essentially all inventory market trading plans count upon just one or kinds. Fundamental investigation is all about an firm's financial status, a unique earnings, and also fiscal property, with its own unique financial debt. The purpose will be to find the inherent value, or so the true price, of the stock market. Technical investigation centers upon the base of inventory reveal expenses and quantities, beyond market actions, and also the path the inventory market is accepting. The purpose will be to use information to earn conjectures concerning the potential motion of this buy cost of the stock market.

Having optimism Stemming in Your frozen Comprehend just how on the two methods is a great quality in a invest or. A whole lot of men and women frequently consider technical analysis since the important thing the both. But some pros mention studying the fundamentals of a particular inventory can set you considerable methods just before your trading friends. Meanwhile, the technical investigation, as several professionals indicate, implements completely different theories and uses a wholly different pair of criteria in comparison to essential investigation. The major purpose, nevertheless, is the fact that there isn't any lone way of choose shares.

In case You are a Newbie investor, then you're Able to find out about the essentials of investing by means of inventory investigation applications offered by most organizations, or by way of online reduction agents. Or-you could register to numerous financial websites that supply enlightening, beneficial stuff and also fantastic details online investment decision. These sites would generally focus about the principles essential to master and also understand the exact workings of this stock market. Most regularly, these internet sites may offer advice about stock trading and investment, dealing methods and notions, relevant inventory picks, as well as of use methods to aid traders proceed their method across the inventory market.

Learning to Be a Amazing Stock Picker can impact Your prosperity accumulation aims to your wonderful degree. If you construct the dexterity into pick stocks, then then you should have increased probability of carrying out exactly the main reason you're while in the inventory market in the first visible spot: wealth. Many small business practitioners, however, realising that investing at the stock market utilizing distinct ways is merely using a notion or even a idea. As a result with the, you're going to be far better off when it will be potential to ascertain exactly the optimal/optimally strategy that may suit your investment design your allowance for risk as well as this timeframe it is possible to in investing along with picking out shares.

Audio Acquiring the Coming Bear Marketplace

We are at a keep Market Place. The inventory Exchange has essentially moved down due to the fact July, and though it really isn't fairly 20% below the past year peaks, just wait around. Can not become trapped at a country of jealousy. The evidence is glaring-the subprime-mortgage and also CDO write-down debacle, a myriad of debt and credit derivatives, even both the banking institutions and fiscal loan haul, exploding realestate bubble, and pathetically high worthiness of these dollar, horrendous federal funding shortages and investing, panicky federal book interest reductions, the departure of Bear Stearns, ineffectual federal re fund stimulus, bond insurance at bankruptcy's door, an financial recession, purchaser investing retrenchment, flat or eroding labour prices, an inflation CPI of +4.3percentage (5%-8percent should this as for example food and energy). Could you say, stagflation? Even radically diminished interest levels are not assisted.

The marketplace runs In cycles. The Last true Recession was in early'90s. Authorities leaders, leaders, even the media, shareholders are more all worried. A catastrophe of optimism is slowly unfolding. Even the excesses of the late'90s Web bubble, also that the newest land bubble, and additionally the spread of junk-mortgages foisted away as AAA-rated debt, even have to get washed out of the system until there exists a return to normalcy.

Trading in a bull Market-place is more straightforward Than buying a bear industry. Many dealers see they may earn currency trading from foreign exchange markets, but nevertheless when there exists a substantial correction penalized whenever the marketplace is bearish they suspend and aren't equipped to swap productively or detect profits inside their very own buying and selling.

To Begin with, as Soon as Market gets fallen, it is Crucial that you simply accept that the business tendency has changed out of bullish to bearish. It has human nature to detect scapegoats or even to find that a"rationale" or to rationalise the undeniable fact the business tendency has shifted. But unless of course the trader accepts the undeniable fact which he's exclusively accountable for swap his own manner out of a foreign exchange marketplace, he will obtain his standing and also find reductions that mount up each single day whilst the market bearish ideas keep on. It will not cover to deny the responsibility of one's trading activities and set the attribute on your broker or your own friend who's contributed you of those "tips" which led on your own losses.

In case You are faced With losses outside of some Sudden fall in prices, and take action really is your own duty to now reevaluate actions to flee the circumstance with profits.

Secondly, Whilst at Bullish markets it is An easy task to exchange just by getting stocks that come initially and just hauling them arriving straight back after a few times to enjoy profits, you can't do precisely the same throughout nominal niches.

In bullish Niches, you exchange together with all the Trend, so long while the tendency remains up, you are still create profits that are easy. On the opposite, at bearish markets, industry goes into bankruptcy, and also trends will be "briefer" in span and so the market place goes to your sideways management, along with prices payable between ranges. Throughout bearish niches, we are a lot more biased in the direction of selection trading rather than buying and selling. So, if you don't know howto change from employing fad dealing to ascertain trading, then then you definitely can be recorded with shortterm fad changes and suffer whipsaws and expel cash fad buying and selling through volatility niches.

Coping with Dealers who have Experienced a Collection of significant current market corrections as 1987 has directed me to complete there's not enough distance to get currency trading by way of volatility niches. The margin of error to get a investing signal will be much lower compared to trading in a bearish industry. I have seen dealers having the power to quickly alter or adapt by trend trading into trading briefer swings over the industry or trading to own the capacity to produce money in their trades. In nominal niches, they truly are happy with lesser profits, however, investing in frequently and at greater quantities. To aid inside their margin of earnings, then they could negotiate the smallest broker provisions potential together with their representatives or even to make use of disregarded on-line dealing platforms.

In bearish Dollar, the trader who scope Commerce will function as the man or woman who's better placed to gain from your briefer and more quicker prices which transpire as shares turned into over-sold and re-trace upwards. Holding private commitment and adapting into extent gambling can boost his chances to create profits throughout minimal markets.

Wall-Street Wont Prove to Bear Economy

Inside My book, Complete of all Bull, " I worry that the Point not to simply take Wall-Street virtually. I'm a few chapters partitioning that the selection of deceptive and confounding avenue directives therefore traders will not be led . On the list of exact bad Street effects on sound investment is its own eternally Favorable stock-exchange bias. You are unable to count up on the-street to frighten you about a negative outlook or greater hazard. In reference into a declining economy as"unstable," in no way the need to accomplish cynical adjectives. Even a market-place Shed can be really a"correction," however a recovery isn't referred to being a"error" as a result Much the stock-exchange fall-off has lasted 4 6 months, even yet The agent study investment test provide is 49 percent Buy, 4 6 percentage Neutral, And just 5% Boost guidelines. Brokerage businesses crank out commissions by attempting to sell to traders secondhand and new stocks and bonds. It's a struggle of attention. Why are they bearish around these goods they want to promote to Clients? Thus do not expect target, attentive advice-even in a tolerate market-from Wall-Street. Even the Street doesn't even admit into this recession. The Government, The Federal

Reserve, is strictly the exact same, always Assessing the prediction positively.

Barron's Summarizes this mentality: "Fundamentally what really is nice, but maybe not to stress, it's going to get much better "

If You hear Wall Road, the Administration," Federal Reserve, and also additionally the cheer-leading media such as CNBC, they all assert we'll soon be past the dilemmas along with progressing yet again from the upcoming 1 / 2 the summer season. They're typical pie-eyed optimists. It really is what you'd count on. But iam telling you that personally, only wait around a two or three months, the pollyanna-ish predictions will start falling, compelling the rally to overdue this season or simply in to early'09. The very first bad issue really isn't the last. It's maybe not an matter of an if there will be considered a hard landing for the market, however rather hard will function as landing. This may be the exact initial purchaser spending-related economic downturn as'9 1 -'9-2. It may last provided that dwelling charges are not gloomy. Election-year doubts along with also the sour drug approaching a year ago working with a fresh government are not a fairly graphic. Finance institutions will probably be chary to provide quite some time, using bad news such as overdue charge debt into your surface. International organization earnings are diminishing. The stock-exchange remains valued in a PE a number of within the long-term fashion lineup, and which isn't re-presenting more revenue quote discounts ahead. It generally seems to me the bear market place will endure properly by means of in 2013 and next yr. Your investment decision has to encircle this careful outlook.

Safe-guard Your Funding

Security of Funding is overriding . Particularly now throughout a worsening market. Investment capital can be overly hard to displace. A 3-5% decrease in worth necessitates a 54% therapeutic to secure right back . The purpose would be not eliminate; avert tripping huge decreases. It's mandatory that you estimate the downside risk of just about every investment decision on your own portfolio. Assume ostensibly just the worst. Usually do not appear to Wall-Street to reveal the lowest cost potential of stocks under evaluation policy. Can it be interested research stories indicate that the up side target, but the lowest cost hazard? Derivatives such as stock choices, phone calls and places, are likely the utmost risk investment, also given the leverage. Individual common stocks really are after. Inventory index funds, exchange traded funds, are somewhat less hazardous. Diversified mutual resources have been lower upon the threat scale. Subsequently it can be trades, accompanied with money around the hazard assortment. Simply get a close look in your expenditure combination. In the approaching bear market place, be sure that your regions are weighted towards the stable ending with the hierarchy.

You will find motives to continue holding Stocks at a portfolio, even also in a market-place falloff. In the event that you're the same as me, you've stocks with healthful benefits that you have to stay for a variety of several years in the future. Attempting to sell these can incur capital gains taxes, and also the tendency will be never to return to re-purchasing those later. Of course in the event that you obey my assistance at complete of all Bull, they're paying decent gains, which represent a substantial revenue flow in your own financial plan. (traditionally, by 1926-2006, a few 41 per cent of the complete stock-exchange yield was originated by dividends, 5 9 percentage in stock price tag appreciation-thus, my give attention to investment paying shares) If these dividend lien had been acquired at low prices, your yield is quite likely to function as potentially approximately ten percentage or much increased. You don't have to devote that. The matter is the fact that stocks entire should signify onto your own portfolio by way of a sector that is dreadful. I believe traders have to reduced their weighting in shares by 30%-50 percent, even when this usually means giving some dividend income to get a quick moment. It's all about keeping your own capital.

Low-Risk Inventory Prepare at a Slumping Economy

Considering that the keep marketplace Performs outside, the Possible cost decrease is more limited in shares using modest PE multiples and also stout investment returns. As an example, they aren't immune to a untapped economy. But, their hazard is quite a bit less than top valuation development shares. Business earnings are still a key service factor inside this specific situation. PE's usually do not imply even when the"E" is not trustworthy. Revenue equilibrium is just a rather significant factor to aid reasonable inventory cost drawback. Even the PE ratio can shrink, however maybe not even when the kick off place is sensible, say that a PE of 10x to 15x. The stocks to get masking a deepening downturn are kinds by which sustainability is not laborious, at which in fact the sales prognosis is immune presenting nations, for example petrol and petroleum pipelines and storage, along with ocean transportation. Incidentally, this type of stock can be really a good expense by means of bull markets too.

Dividend return is just another important buttress. It has really a symptom of monetary balance, amazing money stream, and also caliber. Like I figure out in Total of both Bull, there exists a primary, positive correlation between dividend rates and earnings increase, dependent on exploration similar to you by Robert D. Arnott. Which is a relationship that is laborious. As time moves, the more complex the payout, the faster the more earnings speed. A $20 inventory that pays $0.80 dividend, a 4 per cent yield, is probably not going to plummet below $10 that is, an 8 per cent yield, whenever the earnings and cashflow are stable. The worst scenario situation is a lot more likely approximately $ 1-2, a 6 percent -7percent yield-the dividend, even in case stable, presents a successful security internet. And a investor should seriously consider purchasing much more stocks in the gloomy amount.

Take Other Defensive Plans

From the current Troubled fiscal outlook, Gold, in my own estimation, really is a fantastic expenditure. Throughout a catastrophe or a very uncertain financial interval, gold represents that a safehaven. The weakening greenback, fiscal institution conditions, and inflation most point out gold for a means to guard the worth of one's own funding. Exchange traded funds (ETFs) are an especially straightforward way to find gold for a product. They truly are a real time play, fastidiously track the amount being spent on goldare traded, and also listed major exchanges. An downside to gold-related ETFs could be that the gains are redeemed as slogans, in no further than 28 percent the 1-5% longterm funding gains tax on inventory respect.

Shorting stocks is Still another defensive measure Throughout a substantial stock-exchange falloff. However, this can be far more insecure, so therefore it will only symbolize a tiny portion of one's investment portfolio. Betting a stock may fall communicates together with the chance of infinite declines due to the fact stocks can rise indefinitely nevertheless only fall . Sometime, volatility, and also broker availability to stocks to to offer outside will be all problems. Identify organization sectors that are planning to be more significantly affected by the recession or other cross-currents on the marketplace. Search businesses that will be definitely the absolute most susceptible. And decide on stocks together with valuations that still possess considerable distance . This process is hard since the shares vulnerable to these risks beforehand are apparent and've already fell, such as from your home construction, broker and banking, and also customer banking organizations. You must become about the very first side and also have sufficient comprehension. At case of shorting, I would recommend cutting off your losses incase the shares proceed around in the inappropriate course and grow by 10 percent. It's actually a restricted leash as the threat is really so jaded. But, shorting can be an easy method to cancel losses in the long duration, top caliber, value-oriented, dividend-paying stock holdings.

Be Prepared to Bear-market

The Most Difficult aspect of bettering Your investment portfolio to have yourself a substantial stock-exchange fall-off will be Recognizing the threatening terms, the home market, which There is worse nonetheless to arise. The investment part is significantly easier, ascertaining The right, flat-rate stock locations that might be marketed to earn money. Even a Significant goal is always to decide on a pile of funds, and on occasion maybe a fluid equal just like A valid currency exchange finance, to relish as the rest of the part of this Market tanks. Bear markets are somewhat deceptive, behaving in a Manner that Disguises the downward ramble. Whenever that there occurs a precipitous autumn, it is Followed with a tiny restoration. It's two measures and upward a single measure, just to Keep you confused also to give false expectation. After keep markets are all Commonly recognized it's also late, what has shrunk. Bear markets continue In phases, and everyone can become harm. But This painful Point has never yet happened. At This Time is about the Previous chance which you Alter your portfolio and then tailor it on the upcoming market.

CHAPTER FOUR

Purchasing Guide into Bear Market Profits

A Straightforward Purchasing Guide Might concentrate Around the optimal/optimally approach to put money into the stock market. This brief investment guide is about investing income to profit whether the stock market is decreasing. At a market. Today, actually only a brand-new invest or could do it.Twice between the outset of calendar year 2000 and 2009, a keep marketplace clawed traders badly. Losses ended up in the trillions. Equally occasions a couple of investors knew howto pay and also earned affluent. They'd been quick the stock-exchange - needed a quick stance. To put it differently, they gamble that the stock-exchange will probably fall.

If You're a Brand-new Invest or this Probably appears silly or illegal for your requirements personally. Perhaps not really so. Shorting or even"selling short" or even"shortselling" has been part of this completely free market place mechanism for rather some time. The overdue Joe Kennedy, dad of John F. Kennedy, understood on it. . And was an active player in the niches at age of this Great Depression. Plus it would appear he abandoned currency.

Customarily you Took a short standing in The stock market by purchasing an inventory your broker borrowed to you personally. Then you waited to get your inventory to decline in expense so you can later on acquire it even more cheap and go back on the borrowed shares. The difference reflects that your own gain. Or, if you also bought PUT inventory choices, which is quite a bet a stock(so) will decline in price tag.

In This Investment Decision Guide we will maintain it Easy and not access to the nuts and bolts of both the aforementioned ways of carrying a quick status while in the stock market. Relatively we will reveal the manner in which you are able to purchase out of the market-place that the brand new and simple way by simply investing in a inventory called an reverse or bear-market trade traded fund (ETF). These shares exchange on significant economies including as for instance some other extra stock broadly speaking traded.

A keep economy ETF Maintains a portfolio of Securities with a quick stance, gambling that deals will probably collapse. Whenever you might have stocks of a market traded finance you possess just a tiny area of the portfolio. So, by possessing stocks at a market ETF which shorts that the stock market. . You receive yourself a concise place. You will sell or purchase stocks at an issue of minutes any-time that the stock market will be available.

Here Is an example Of how to invest As an inventory market BEAR (the one who stocks that deals will likely fall). To get a fresh invest or you get 100 stocks in SDS, a keep market fund that accommodates the S&P 500 Index with just two into at least one leverage. Let us mention that you simply cover $40 per talk to get a whole price of 4000. You might acquire 10 stocks or tens of thousands of tens of thousands but only pay out $10 commission by means of a low cost agent.

Per month following the Inventory market as Quantified from the S&P five hundred Index (that reflects the market

) is down 10 percentage). Your SDS stock with 2 to at least one leverage should be up roughly 20 percentage approximately even $ 8 to somewhere around $ 4-8. It will be likely to get, assert sell to get a profit of somewhere around 20 percent. The method is the fact that easy.

What's not simple Is the time your purchase, as Thus in the event the stock exchange market extends up once you obtain SDS, then the inventory will soon return. The buyer also has to become mindful of these hazards involved with fiscal leverage (such as two to inch) and gambling from the stock market. It truly is more frequently than it truly is downward. But this isalso in a market.

You'll find lots of Maintain market place ETFs. Get Acquainted using them and also the way in which in that they exchange. You have the capability to receive your toes wet to get a handful hundred dollars. Inch final trick out with the investment guide for grips: Don't buy these stocks being a long-lasting obtain and retain. If you choose a concise standing also it goes contrary to you, put out at just a small discount and also live to play the next day. A bull economy like one who commenced in March of 2009 can possibly be barbarous in the event that you're a bear.

Paying for - Organizing On The Following Bear Current Market

That is the'Tea Leaves' notification us"The sky is falling?" Nomore waitpatiently, shake off the cupagain. . "The sky is the limitation?" Today that's the answer each of us would really like!

After trading and investing were simple, we now May cover a trip into some Reader to get a few bucks and also know exactly what exactly the near future holds. Unfortunately, in case you ask three associates what their leaves are all stating, you acquire about three completely different professional remarks. Psychotherapy is not their strong suit.

To Begin with, I've Not Ever produced any folks Prophecies regarding the upcoming direction of this current market or even the industry and also do not mean to begin with today. Also, I'm perhaps not even a stock-exchange Bear, I'm maybe not even a Bull, so I truly do not involve any absurd switches to slap which create all types of crazy noises to let you get - get - buy, together side my own dart plank is actually a dart plank as opposed to an inventory set device. I truly do not imagine Chicken minor was a wonderful prognosticator and now I don't actually feel the earth will finish tomorrow. But, twenty five years of market seeing experience informs me are certainly a couple matters that traders need to surely be concerned about.

Permit out The generalized and Sensationalized noise about just about every present current market sign up down or up. We are going to depart this on the talking-heads with their television cameras along with cup of java renders; nonetheless, it provides them some thing to perform and averts them outside of us. We desire to focus on the huge photo, the substantial occasions, and also how these incidents will be likely to have an effect on the marketplace last but not least the upcoming management of the forex marketplace. Ideally, you have the capacity to to get some perception concerning what could be about that occurs and strategies to get ready yourself.

Let Us Take a Look in a Couple Of the important Factors.

For instance: Un Employment, Foreclosures, Housing Market Place, Home Finance Loan Crisis, the Greenback, the EU, and Gold, Only to List a Couple.

It's not Rocket Science, simple ordinary Sense claims the home market wont rise before foreclosures certainly are no further a issue and foreclosures may last to become problem as long since unemployment is not advancing. Together with 25 percentage of house owners currently up side in their own mortgage (invest the property is currently value) the gentle at the close of the tubing for foreclosures continues to be attached with a sizable moving item using a rather loud whistle.

As You May Be Aware, The Home Finance Loan disaster Didn't move off. Allowed, dozens of junk commissions that were jammed and jammed from your bull, ended upn't paid total with all the fulfilled homeowners, so the cash stays owed; nonetheless there clearly was just a small alteration within the technique of bookkeeping inorder they seem superior on newspaper now. Why don't we proceed into an alternative indicator.

Together with commissions and foreclosures Being a Back-ground, today simply take under account the buy price . As you understand gold is around a rip plus has been float approximately $1400 for every ounce. You should ask yourself, what might cause that? Recognizing that supply and demand finally lays the transferring cost, the evident raised demand for your own prized steel is the most likely as your dental practitioner is still tremendously busy satisfying your Jeweler hasbeen on the lookout for greater targeted visitors. Therefore that leaves just one sensible choice. Concern within the currency, the Green spine notably, and also much more notably, its own worth. Neglect the pair rookie dealers that jump in paying for gold at the current prices anticipating the purchase price will soon twice instantly plus they'll acquire rich rapidly, should they usually do not eliminate their money, then chances are they are going to shed it somewhere else. It's their destiny. That which we are focused on could be the large picture. Together side the huge film in forms us that this is not a excellent index on industry to state at the very least.

There is an elderly widow,"Should you Desire the facts, then comply with the money."

In Addition to this Currency worries, worried Gold-snatching shareholders, or even Mr. Bernanke along with also his eldest helicopter distributing green springs to everyone however you and that I personally, what wouldbe exactly the insiders carrying out?

You understand, people who should be'From that the Understand' and in addition have a deal on what exactly the industry is quite likely to do along with exactly what affect that could have about the marketplace, not to mention the influence it is likely to own about their organization stock-price. I could believe I truly do find it fascinating which giant businesses such as Microsoft, Hewlett Packard and lots of more have lately manufactured the advice from searching hiring and for prominent economists out of locations like Harvard. Why can they make such abrupt curiosity about academics?

Other than That, Let's us determine exactly what the actual Insiders do by using their very own inventory exchange.

Insiders, Clearly, really are an company's Supervisors, supervisors and greatest share holders. Those who buy yourself a first hand look at the dictates, projections, earnings, etc.. They truly are also demanded by law to almost immediately report into the SEC each time they will have obtained or offered stocks of their businesses' inventory exchange.

Well do you know what? They have been around a sale Trend. Endorsing the shares of these businesses' buy within an record-pace maybe not seen as ancient 2007. Permit me to remind youthat that was just a few of short months before this awesome Recession started off.

Vickers Weekly Insider Report assesses the Insider statistics per week additionally calculates a proportion of the number of shares which These trained respondents also have given this week in to the total amount they've ordered. Vickers Weekly Statesthroughout the previous 4 decades (forty years now) this ratio H AS shrunk between 2 and 2.5 to inch. Any examining 2.5-to-1 can be a Above-average rate of attempting to sell into this insiders, and may even be an eyeopener for the own investor.

Today Keep in Your Mind People insiders Have Been Selling at recording rate in ancient 2007 and keep maintaining your breath ahead of analyzing what this sell-to-buy ratio was in December," 2010. 7.07-to-1. In other words company insiders on balance have been encouraging significantly more than simply 7 stocks to get every single that they're acquiring. Only to prove that this really isn't an apology, two weeks ago the sell-to-buy ratio has since been 5.29-to-1, additionally has increased ever since afterward.

The following variable that the individual investor Must recall while believing'big picture' is Bear Markets. I'm mindful of, no one would like take under account the business sucking and jelqing the average of 29 percentage of these value out of the investment account having to await a couple decades to return straight back . But just like it not, for its previous a hundred decades there is been a bear-market within the typical of every about three and a half (3.5) years. They are across like Id, they continue a mean of 18 weeks, so then abandon investors anticipating a several decades to find the investment decision account balance return into this shameful. Need I remind one personally, the closing Bear market place commenced in 2007? You're doing the mathematics.

Therefore imagine in the event that you really do? I'm Not suggesting you Call your broker and also sell-out, also I don't want to seem just like Chicken Little, it's maybe not my individuality. But, I believe that you should pay careful attention into this market indexes, twist the ceases and get ready to get the worst, and also expect for the very best. As soon as I authored the books'Charting and Technical examination' and'wise practice paying for', " this present marketplace circumstance is precisely what I desired to prepare for the respective buyer. And the best way to avoid the dredging of portfolio decimation caused by current market declines. 1 additional crucial thing to stay in your mind could be that the economic Advisor won't enable you to promote. Shielding your investment bucks is merely your duty. So, perhaps instruct your self investment and also be knowledgeable about providing your investment decisions or keep your hard-won income safe and sound from your financial institution. It's the choice.

Fundamental Investor Manual into Unsightly Bear Markets

Generally in the majority of decades most volatility go up..the Stock market consists of upward. A whole lot of time the inventory market is not genuine interesting, together with stock deals shifting pretty. The large part of time we are at a bull market place where stocks proceed greater. In a stand marketplace costs collapse. When stock prices are emerging which is the exception that clearly receives people's attention rate.

This Is Especially Authentic today, as Countless impatient investors have their fiscal stocks drifting shares (inventory funding) from 401(k) and IRA ideas. This is the basic Invest or Manual to continue to keep markets of the past. How poor possess stock costs dropped Sooner, and also how exactly can this review to 2007 2009?

In Quantifying inventory Market-place or Normal stock operation, we will pay attention to the DOW JONES INDUSTRIAL AVERAGE (DJIA). This stock indicator could be your oldest and also the very widely used among shareholders, usually called the DOW. It permits you to realize the way the big penny stocks are doing, also essentially signals how shares are doing.

Traditionally, Shares have returned Ten percentage each year within the very long haul. As soon as the Dow falls 5 per cent each week, then your vast most traders eliminate cash. In case it drops by 20 per cent or even more than a period frame we are at a market, and also most stock traders (besides that the infrequent speculator) discard dollars.

History may provide Us a feeling of View, also be the very simple invest or handbook. Today let's take a take a look at some really horrible inventory markets.

The keep marketplace That started in 1929 was that the Worst in Western heritage, with all the Dow decreasing 8-9 percentage throughout its own de crease in 1932. It required two years for inventory prices then go straight back with their former highs of 1929. An important reason supporting the business wreck: Extra financial sway. Traders had bid up stock deals together with borrowed income.

1973-1974: In underneath 2 years that the Stock Exchange fell 45 percent. This bear market place was accompanied closely by increasing interest rates plus greater inflation.

2000 2002: " The Dow fell 38 per cent, however Growth stocks got (specially hitech shares). The NASDAQ Composite Index fell 78 per cent within three years. Stocks that had turned into similar to a rocket dropped to earth as a rock. Invest or speculation created excess stock prices notably in parts related to private computer systems, the world wide web and cellular telephones.

2007 2009: Later raising for Somewhere around five many years, stock Costs commenced falling at the autumn of 2007. Per year later financial tragedy happened like a catalyst and also the market took a nose dive. In early 2009 inventory charges had been down above 50 per cent. The planet's fiscal strategy, also markets around the whole world, ended up in acute problem.

After more extortionate financial sway and Speculation performed an important function. Leading finance organizations, other companies, investors and homeowners engaged inside this match. Monetary leverage is just investing in borrowed income. Some major Wall-Street firms transferred into incredulous extremes. Many individuals on main-street collapsed way too, according to land possessions with really modest if down any money.

To sum This up, the Bear marketplace that started In late 2007 may be your worst as the Great Depression. The ending can not be properly predict. Traders normally concentrate on 6 months after on. When, and just whenthey find a brighter future they will start paying for and send stock costs larger. In case the development carries on, then a fresh bull market place has created.

Currency Markets Purchasing Manual

The Stock-exchange Is full of Investment opportunities occasionally. Some-times currency markets investing can reverse a couple investors reductions in over 50 percentage, such as in 2000 2002 and 2008. After is an inventory investment guide to simplify your expenditure encounter and also to help you for earning money stock investment without even sacrificing lots of it into keep markets.

Like a basic Investment guide, inventory Investing involves both industry timing and stock assortment. Byway of example, you get X Y Z monetary LOW in March of both 2009 and promote it high-a handful months later.

That Is a Great Approach to Make Money out of The stock market in the event that you're able to have it performed regularly. Few dealers ' are effective at detecting such expense chances (decision) and executing transactions productively in the ideal time (market time). That's called controversy plus it demands commitment and expertise, energy and time.

This is just another Simple investment guide incite. Speculation is not a filthy term. . But real investment chances are not simple to comprehend. The chances are often contrary to the in experienced investor. Here is the way to make money from the stock market and never lending back it every time a bear-market (lowering inventory deals) claws Wall-Street.

Give Up-on Searching for Inventory market Investment chances (prices), and also pay attention to advertise timing. Sustain your niche period general in nature by minding the Dow Jones Industrial Average (the DOW) over weekly basis.

Do not stay 100 percent Committed to stocks on Your broker accounts. As additional investors can attest to, a bear-market will wipeout countless economy profits immediately. At the occasion that you get rid of 50 percentage you've got to double your hard earned money to merely get right back again to. Here's the effortless method to manage advertise timing.

Keep approximately 1 / 2 Your capital out of Stocks that monitor your stock-exchange broadly speaking with the spouse of your own accounts. By Method of Instance, SPY tracks the S&P 500 Index and also D-IA tracks the DOW. That's the impartial place.

Provided that the Inventory Exchange is stable Or climbing stay only 50% committed to shares. If a bear industry is out of the info (after a 20% decrease from your DOW) move more cash to stocks. As shares are still drop your stock paying for.

Right at the Start you Want to Receive a target and In addition, the guts of one's personal convictions. Byway of example, you will need to become ready to obtain stocks at the market place drops with a purpose to become 90 percent spent and when the market falls fifty per cent.

In case you can't ever Compel to Get Stocks if a person are still selling, inventory investing is not for you personally.

Around the Reverse side, You've Got to Start Selling stocks after a large installation, to get in touch with your impartial status of 50 percent. Economy timing is not a science, but it's an art form which really needs your consideration.

Stock investment or Developing a inventory Investment does not involve expertise inside the stock market. You don't need to manually choose stocks all on your or just take on excess possibility to buy shares. After is really a conventional beginner guide to stock investing for beginners.

Whatever You Would like to Learn More about this Stock exchange should you create your primary stock expenditure would be that inventory price ranges range. Stocks commerce online transactions, also if held to its longterm shares have made yields of somewhere around ten per cent each yr. Around the shorter-term the marketplace experiences cycles called bull markets (climbing charges) and maintain markets (decreasing rates).

Nearly All this Instant Bull markets Prevail and several traders make funds. In bears markets which the vast bulk of traders eliminate dollars, as most shares drop value.

Purchasing Novices should not be around Attempting to choose stocks which may out perform the stock exchange market broadly speaking. Inventory investing, specially investing in beginners, if really be thinking about creating an inventory expense without so much as speculating and taking on significant threat.

The Simplest Approach To Buy stocks with no Speculating is to invest in business growth funding: market traded funds (ETFs), along with mutual capital. From the situations you make an inventory investment decision from paying for shares. Afterward you definitely have just a tiny percentage of the huge portfolio of stocks which will be managed for you personally and also the remaining part of the traders who have shares.

To Put Money into Stocks through an ETF You're Going to need a broker accounts. Inventory mutual capital might be found in quite a few manners: in the shape of a investment pro, in a 401k-type prepare, in an agent account, or even simply by dealing with a no-load fund organization.

Unless You have obtained a Investment adviser You also are going to desire to decide on your budget to invest in. Being an total manual to buying newbies, it's advisable to to receive going investing using a substantial stock indicator finance.

By Method of Instance, stock Emblem SPY will be An ETF that monitors a considerable stock indicator, the S&P 500 Index. A number of mutual-fund organizations supply S&P 500 Index funding far too. In any event, they have been an inventory investment that tracks the operation of all 500 of the greatest stocks (large cap shares) at the us.

In good occasions in Bull markets, you're Heading to make funds. Some-times and maintain markets such as at 2008, be prepared you'll expel money combined side virtually everyone else which left the determination to put money into shares.

The Awesome Truth about investing at an Stock index fund which monitors the inventory marketthe most of the shares proceed upwards in worth. In addition, unlike most people who pick out shares to overcome the present market place, you don't need to sweat the danger that you simply chose ill. . Leading to larger than ordinary reductions.

Today That You Know The way to Buy Stocks to share inside the stock-exchange with out undue threat, you're getting to need to learn regarding investment program. After you comprehend just how exactly to stop massive declines in keep markets, then you're much before numerous dealers.

Investing at the Stock Trade

On the Last Couple of Decades the inventory market Has made significant reductions. Some short-term traders have lost a wonderful piece of money. A few brand new inventory dealers believe that this and also start to become quite doubtful about turning out to be today.

In case You are Contemplating investing from the Stock exchange it truly is critical you realize the manner by which the markets run. Just about every the marketplace and monetary advice that the newcomer is bombarded with will probably render them confused and overwhelmed.

The Stock-exchange is a routine expression utilized To consult with an area where inventory organizations has been bought and sold. Businesses problems inventory to finance new gear, and purchase different organizations, enlarge their organization and present brand new products, etc.. The shareholders who obtain this inventory finally possess a talk of this supplier. In case the business does properly exactly the buy price tag of this inventory increases. At case the organization does not prosper the inventory value declines. At case the fee that you simply sell your stock to get is much more than you taken care of it, then then you have got made dollars.

Whenever You Purchase stock In a company that You discuss from the losses and earnings with the provider until you offer your own stock or your business is out of business. Numerous reports have proven that prolonged haul stock possession has become one of the most top investment decision programs for lots of .

Folks purchase stocks onto a proposal out of the Close friend, a mobile call from the broker, or even perhaps a recommendation from an television analyst. They invest in throughout a effective industry. Subsequent to the later commences to diminish that they sell and fear to get a discount. This could be the standard horror story we all hear out of people who do not own some investment program.

Previous to committing your Hard-won money to The stock market it's going to induce one to consider the advantages and pitfalls of executing so. You have to get a investment program. This tactic will even define exactly what when to get and also when you are going to market it.

Record of the Stock-exchange

Over Two 100 Decades Straight Back personal Banks began initially to market inventory to raise dollars to expand. This really is a brand-new approach to invest in and also an easy method for the rich to acquire wealthier. In 1792 twenty-five significant retailers consented to earn a market-place known as the New York Stock Exchange (NYSE). They consented to match with daily on WallStreet and sell and purchase stocks.

By the mid 1800s The U.S. Was experiencing accelerated enlargement. Organizations began initially to market inventory to raise dollars for its growth essential to meet the increasing requirement for his or her products and services. Even the women and men who ordered this stock grew to become a part proprietors of the company and contributed at the sales or lack in their supplier.

A New Type of purchasing began to Arise When traders realized that they would promote their stock to additional folks. This can be where speculation began initially to impact an investor's decision to sell or purchase and also led how to enormous changes instock prices.

To Begin with Investing from the stock market Was limited to this exact affluent. Currently inventory possession has identified it's way to most industries of this whole world.

What is a Inventory?

A inventory Certificate Is a Part of newspaper Declaring you own part of the business. Organizations promote inventory to invest in progress, engage men and women, promote, etc.. In general, the sale of stock assistance businesses develops. Even the women and men that get the stock reveal in the losses or earnings of this supplier.

Signs of stock Is Broadly Speaking pushed By shortterm speculation concerning the firm surgeries, services, goods, etc.. It truly is this speculation that influences an investor's decision to sell or purchase and exactly what costs will be all appealing.

The Business Enterprise raises Currency throughout the Main business. Here really is actually the Very First Public Offering (IPO). Subsequently that the inventory is traded at the secondary market place (that which we predict the stock market) when human investors or traders purchase and sell the shares into a another. The firm is not affected with virtually any profit or loss in your leading trade.

Tech and the Net has produced the inventory Promote readily available into the people. Computers also have made investment from the stock market fairly easy. Market and Business information could be had nearly everywhere on the planet. The World Wide Internet has brought an enormous New collection of traders into the stock market which collection maintains growing .

Bull-market - Bear-market

Anybody Who Has been following the inventory Seeing or exchange television information is the most likely proficient in regards to the terms bull-market along with bear-market. Exactly what exactly do they signify?

A bull market Is Distinguished by steadily Increasing prices. The Marketplace Is booming and companies are often getting A gain. Most traders believe that this trend tends to last for a short time. From Contrast a bear market place is just one wherever costs have been decreasing. The Industry would be Likely in a reduction and many associations are undergoing issues. Now The shareholders are pessimistic concerning the upcoming sustainability of this Stock market. Since Traders' attitudes frequently induce their openness to. Obtain or promote them trends normally overtake themselves before Significant outside events interfere to make a reversal of perspective.

At a bull marketplace Exactly the buyer anticipates to Purchase ancient and keep the inventory right up until it has reached it's quite high. Demonstrably Forecasting the low and high will be impossible. Since most traders Really are"bullish" which they generate significantly more profit the rising bull industry. They are Prepared to invest additional cash Whilst the stock is still rising and also recognize Greater benefit.

Investing in a Maintain Economy Interrupts the Very Ideal Chance of declines considering that the trend in downhill and there is zero end insight. A expenditure plan inside cases like this could possibly be brief selling. Short sale is attempting to sell a stock you never possess. It's likely to produce arrangements together with your broker to find this carried out. You might in consequence be borrowing stocks in the agent to sell from your expectation of paying for back them after whenever the fee gets fallen. You will benefit from your gap from the 2 expenses. Still another way to receive yourself a keep market is purchasing real money shares. All these are shares like utility organizations that are not influenced from the market recession or companies that market their product all through all financial problems.

Brokers

Customarily Investors purchased and marketed Inventory through large brokerage homes. They left a mobile call for the representative who relayed their order into the industry . These representatives additionally furnished their products and services since inventory advisers to individuals who knew very little in the market. These individuals now depended upon their own broker to guide them compensated a large expense in commissions and fees because of this. The arrival of this net internet has led in some other type of agent residences. These businesses deliver on the web accounts at which you may possibly sign into and get and market stocks from everywhere you may locate an internet relationship. They do not provide you with some business info and simply provide dictate implementation. The internet buyer may find some amazing deals whilst the associates of this brand new strain of virtual broker homes compete on the organization!

Blue-chip Shares

Enormous nicely equipped businesses that have Exhibited great increase and sustainability, dividend payout, and good quality products and services are called bluechip shares. They have been on average the pioneers of the company, are available for quite some time, and are considered among the most secure investments. Blue-chip stocks are included inside the Dow Jones Industrial Average, an indicator written of thirty-two companies which can be pioneers in their business enterprise teams. They truly are highly favored by individual and institutional shareholders. Bluechip stocks lure investors who are enthusiastic about consistent profits and increase as well as equilibrium. They are infrequently susceptible into the purchase price volatility of distinct stocks along with also their talk prices will typically be more than different sorts of stock trading. The draw back of chips is the fact that as a result of these stability they'll not appreciate as fast compared to smaller sized stocks which can be more upfront.

Very Cheap Shares

Very Cheap Stocks Are Extremely Inexpensive stocks. And therefore are incredibly insecure. They have been typically issued by businesses without a permanent listing of endurance or stability.

The appeal of Penny stock is that their non Price tag. Even though possibilities are contrary to it, even whenever business may input a rise trend the share-price can leap quite fast. They have been typically preferred by the insecure investor.

Profits Shares

Cash Flow Stocks are all Stock that normally Cover greater than ordinary volatility. They truly are well-known firms such as phone or utilities organizations. Cash flow shares are quite favored by most of the current buyer who'd really like to truly have the inventory to get quite some time and accumulate the proceeds and who is not interested at an gain from share price tag.

Really worth Shares

Sporadically a Organization's earnings and expansion Potential indicate it is share-price should be much higher than it truly is currently trading whatsoever. These stock are believed to be more price shares. For the large part, the present investors and market have ignored them. The buyer that purchases an worth stock anticipates the market place will probably soon comprehend exactly what a bargain it will be and commence to get. This will drive the talk price tag.

Defensive Shares

Defensive Shares Are issued by most companies in Organizations who demonstrate good efficiency in markets that are poor. Food items and usefulness organizations have been all rules.

Overall economy Stage

On the List of most Famous marketplace quotations Is:"Buy Low - Sell High". In order continuously powerful from the stock exchange one necessitates tactic, subject, understanding, and tools. We'll have to grasp our tactic and stick to this. This can prevent individuals from turning out to be diverted by fear, emotion, and on occasion possibly greed.

On the List of Exact Well Known investing Strategies employed by"expense pros" is market-timing. This can be actually the hard work to predict long term fees from preceding economy operation. Forecasting inventory prices is becoming a problem for way too long since men and women are stocks. The chance to get or market an inventory is situated on various fiscal indexes predicated on industry identification, inventory charts, and assorted intricate mathematical and pc dependent calculations.

There Are Lots of dangers Associated in Investing from the stock exchange market. Recognizing these threats exist should be one of those matters that an investor is always attentive to. The cash you buy from the stock market is not ensured. To take one example,, you can buy a inventory expecting a certain dividend or speed of share value development. In case the corporation undergoes financial problems it may possibly perhaps not meet your investment or price growth requirements. At case the company is from business then you will probably eliminate what you put in within it. On account of the doubt of this outcome, you suffer a specific volume of hazard after you obtain yourself a stockexchange.

Shares disagree from the Entire amount of Dangers they present. By way of instance, Web stocks also have established themselves to turn into more speculative compared to shares.

1 danger is the volatility reaction to News things in regards to the organization. Predicated along how the traders interpret the brand-new item, they are changed to sell or purchase the stock exchange. If lots of these traders begin to sell or purchase in the specific very same moment it is going to create the purchase price to drop or increase.

1 strong Technique to Take Care of risk is diversification. This usually means spreading out your investments over various stocks within many different niche businesses. Keep in your mind that the expression:"Don't put your eggs all at the specific very same jar".

As traders We Must Track down this Our"possibility Tolerance". Possibility tolerance is the emotional and financial power to trip out a decline available on the market without selling and repainting in a reduction. Once we define that we create sure to not enlarge our investments beyond .

Positive Aspects

The Exact same forces Which contribute threat Into investment from the stock market make potential that the huge profits many traders enjoy. It's appropriate the fluctuations in the market-place cause reductions as well as profits however in case you have a proven prepare and stay to it in the future you're going to be considered a success!

The Entire World Wide Internet has Make money in The stock market an opportunity for not exactly every one. The prosperity of internet info, articles, and also inventory quotes provides typical man the exact same capacities that were currently readily available to just inventory brokers. You can forget will the trader needs to have in contact an agent with this particular information or maybe to place orders to sell or purchase. We've got virtually instantaneous accessibility to the accounts and also the capacity to place on the web requests in minutes. This brand new freedom has ushered into brand new masses of investors that are optimistic. Yet this is in fact maybe not just a random procedure of purchasing and marketing stock trading. We're needing of the policy for picking out an proper inventory as well as period and energy to get and promote to have the ability to develop an earnings.

Day-trading

Day-trading would be your Strive to buy and market Stock inside a quite brief period of time. Your afternoon dealer anticipates to revenue the short-term fluctuations in a stock's cost. It'd not be rare for every single day trader to sell and get exactly the specific same inventory in an issue of a few moments or even to get and market exactly the specific same stock often situations daily.

Day dealers sit of pc screens All-day looking for shortterm movement at a market exchange. They then strive to become in to the move before it yells. The genuine day trader will not have an inventory immediately on account of the chance of an occasion or advice thing tripping the stock exchange to undo route. It needs extreme attention to monitor exactly the moment by minute movement of stocks that are many.

Day-trading provides a Great Deal of risk As a result of doubt with this market behavior within the quick period. The tiniest governmental or financial advice may result in an inventory to change immensely and bring about losses that are unforeseen.

If a person says that The business will be Volatile, therefore it will not indicate the market place is entirely arbitrary. That can be one of those essential tenets to chart and set that the trend-lines; yet the most essential measure whenever you perform by way of the many research graphs and examine substance to produce the predictions in regards to the talk industry. Trade do not move lightly upward at an excellent terminal leadership.

They are an Essential tool in Technical analysis for the style identification and confirmation. Figuratively speaking, it is really a searchable lineup attracted between two significant things onto a chart. It can stretch from the foreseeable future to be the lineup of service or immunity. It's going to help discover the trend in the in addition to how provides the exact picture of potential parts of service and immunity. Since it gives the managing of this industry motion, it provides a most important factor in virtually any evaluation.

This is an guide to financial spread gambling. Generally speaking, it truly is all about a few methodical system of exchange stocks, including an step-by-step guide to work with your on-line share dealing account; the way to buy and keep maintaining top generating stocks; both the little and great thematic investment; launching with the prevent loss restricts to pick the profits.

"An Up-trend Is Distinguished by Successively increased drops, whilst the regular pull-backs form exerts higher extremities" The opposite does occur in a downtrend. To construct a trendline, then an individual should fully grasp at which in fact the business is guided. At an increasing economy, it might be constructed underneath the successive highs made by the pull-backs below the bull movements. Sometime at a market, it has really a downward incline lineup linking the shirts with the bear market occasions.

Because of the proper Comprehension and Interpretation, it truly is critical to get paid profits on the marketplace. The master plan which fits towards this existing feeling of this market place must be adopted. Byway of example, in the event the is transferring upward, a trader need ton't start using a call call spread. This type of movement could possibly be more counterproductive.

Even Though investment About the premise of appropriate Understanding of this trend-lines can result in good profits, the threat of dropping each the investment decision cannot be eliminated. You must beat the proper framework of the mind to swap in compliance with all the necessity of the instant.

"To get a Prosperous trader, you Must Know markets stronger compared to contest " Recognizing that the trend-line together with an all-inclusive comprehension of specialized test would be the methods to promote profits, even though averting unanticipated drawbacks of declines.

Once and Recognizing it, would be the Allimportant endeavor of a analyst. Now a pull-back to an up sloping fashion lineup in a bull-market could be your indicator to get your own purchasing chance, even whenever you've got missed the very first movement. Know every time a style line has been brokenup, you will find the substantial indication of a change at the direction with this fashion. Subsequent to industry closes, having endorsed industry an assortment of instances to find yourself a functioning with the bull market place, it is the the indication the specialized trader must learn more about the impending risk.

Trend-lines are all Exemplary Areas to Start Trading items using a rather low hazard entrance. A comprehension with this tendency lineup usually suggests a fracture with this trend which delivers you having a exit hint. Their value and legitimacy depends upon about the total amount of that time period the price rolls it.

1 important advantage of Style lines Is They permit one to pick astute Options for your own trade. They aid distinguish involving emotional decisions from analytical decisions. They always maintain you around the perfect side with the market. In just about any predicament profits stinks due of amazing choices shot in the perfect instant.

But on WallStreet, the Meaning of the keep Economy is if charges drop 20% under current prices. Broadly, charges will probably collapse much more afterward in a market. Inside this time, day-trading becomes quite catchy. For the seasoned traders. This is due throughout a bear market, volatility climbs. This growth in volatility could be what which produces trading quite difficult throughout those days. Traders have been understood to expel all of their trading capital if there exists a bear industry.

Exactly what A-day Trader perform to Become ready to get A industry decrease? The absolute greatest thing you might certainly do is start out paying awareness of certain signs that'll make it possible for one to learn what route a is contributed to. Indicators you should be watching to get will be price tag, volume, 52 week drops, 52 week lows, the Tri-N, the reduction point etc.. Once you know that which direction a is led in, you have the capacity to to earn the essential moves to safeguard your own profits.

The Very First thing you should perform would be scale Back position measurements. Trade 50 percent of what you were residing whenever the economy was around the up swing. The target here is to store just as much capital as you can. If you should be the form of afternoon dealer who keeps positions instantly, be sure which they're modest. Maintaining places sets you in higher danger of economy change.

1 factor to bear in Your Head is that Even though business is determined by the reduction, it's likely to earn a profit from a market. There will be a couple times when stocks will closed onto the upside down. Through the duration of the last tolerate market not exactly 40 percentage of the trading days shut into the upside down. It truly is easy to comprehend when there exists a opportunity to obtain therefore you may take advantage of it. Ordinarily, the downward trend is simply likely to last for way too long before it takes a concise pause. This brief dip is going to become your possibility to develop an earnings. Just don't forget the dip will undoubtedly be more short. It will gradually stay static inside its own downward trend.

It Is Additionally a good Notion to swap Various tools within this sort of marketplace. Don't Count entirely on person Shares. Take into account buying and selling ETF's or stock index stocks instead. Generally, it is Exceptionally viable to exchange through a bear industry. Only be sure You realize more about the disadvantages therefore you might avoid their store.

CHAPTER FIVE

Financial Freedom for A Stock Trader

I Assume That in Case You Just Click the After record that you are with the desire to bring in profit stock industry. Inside my own experienceI suggest that the most worthwhile approach to earn stock-exchange online is via means of buying and selling. However, to be honest with you personally, to become loaded fast through inventory afternoon trading is equally impossible, and also considerate to trust that. Like a beginner, you have must know from flooring upward and may reward your fiscal liberty. These tips would be the gold principles for people that like to swap inside stock market.

As Everyone Probably Knows, Favorable Longterm inventory Investment can create profits along using the product range Approximately ten percentage per annum in the event you keep on a distinct much healthier stock selection. While inventory trading Could Produce a sound profit out of an trading day trading Period or maybe shorter. Thus, if You are ready to perfect exactly the pro skill daily trading, then it goes to become successful in getting long-term expenditure.

Due to This Range of business Registered nowadays, stock-exchange provides a number of selections and opportunities. This trend Gives chances for dealers to"refine" and"infusion" probably the most lucrative stock picks. You'll Locate wide distribute of volatility which eventually become "hot inventory" every

Week Obey the fast changing Business weather, for example green, biotech vitality, on line press, mass communication and healthcare businesses.

The Most Essential Factors I Would like to advocate Are the volatility and liquidity of this stock in the event that you're performing trading. In laymen interval, larger liquidity indicates big buying and selling frequency whereas big volatility compatible elevated trading budget assortment. Neglect these inventory picks together with nominal cost movement as opposed to catching eye chunk of traders.

Still another mentality Ought to Be embraced would be to be more Continuous in executing the own trading region. Elect to get a great and adequate plan, utilize essentially the most important stuff and stick using the basic principles to get the good. I'll urge you may be elastic to control unforeseen circumstances, however don't just transform your strategy, but this will cause the catastrophic effect.

Lastly, though together with all the Aid of advancement tech stock-trading platform or even hedging strategy, a person needs to appreciate that buying and selling from the unstable and exceptionally changing inventory exchange entails selected amount of threat. You can lose it nevertheless, you still are unable to wholly expel risk shooting. My private information is that n't calls for your personal emergency publication together with buying and selling. Trade with your excess cash, that may even allow you to earn bold but accurate conclusion at significant moment.

Folks Are Continuously Watching out to get a Means to flee out of the corporate jungle and avoid investing hours in work. Many might really like to be able to just work in your home and devote more quality time together with their nearest and dearest associates as well as family members. However about generating the option to begin a livelihood at your home lots of are scared they'll not get enough money to call home so that any movements away from the pit of debt will most likely be shortlived. In the event you mention to all those individuals they would become an inventory broker and also operate in your home they simply do not think that you.

Properly, it really is legitimate. Because of improvements In modern technology and just how firm is now completed it truly is very likely to run a booming stock broking corporation in the contentment of of one's home, only having a laptop as well as a couple professional pc program. This really is due, specially, towards this money exchange additionally described because the forex market place. Using the forex current market you are able to start trading international exchange with relatively little expertise and training, what exactly is it requires a couple of hours of time daily to produce in to a forex trader while still supplying appreciable benefits (broadly speaking in the figure range), hence supplying you all of the monetary flexibility you want.

Previous to you Put away the Path Growing financial flexibility by operating at house you ought to undertake some essential currency trading coaching. The absolute best way to complete this will be always to wait for a couple of the various inventory broking classes available on the market. Within an stock exchange broking course you are going to have the ability to speak with experienced dealers who have undergone a lot of succeeding over the money markets. You are going to possess the capacity to discuss together with the top most useful way to begin setting your company and figure out in the absolute most useful means of earning trades along with the best way to offset your own dangers. Additionally you will see that most profits generated of your FX trades are taxfree from britain, providing you using a far bigger fiscal incentive for always a stockbroker.

Organizing Danger and Reward

Therefore Only What'll soon be threat and advantage? In Lifetime you can find a number of potential risks you need to choose. Crossing the trail is just a threat. Providentially, a clear large part of enough moment, a person can restrain this hazard. You look both ways before crossing the trail. The exact same goes for investment. Paying for has inherent potential risks yet an individual could (for a limited scope) restrain the threat. Your fiscal freedom will be closely associated with just how much the right time you decide since it'll ascertain the amount of benefit you are going to garner out of your investments. Every thing boils right down from exactly what a few people now call"the sleeping variable". How effectively do you want to sleep soundly in the nighttime?

Can you like maybe not worry on your Own investments that will ensure it is feasible that you sleep far better? Or are you really the aggressive kind that wants to choose to your celebrities together with your investments which will force you to forget that a evening or 2 sleep? It's mandatory that you choose your tolerance to benefit and risk. By the fiscal world that's named an person's risk tolerance. Just how would you suffer hazard? Whenever you take up a retirement account or a broker account to start investing, then you are going to be filling a schedule that includes many inquiries lots of who may be geared at detecting your risk tolerance and also a couple will most likely be specific at detecting your time and effort horizon. In other words, just what are you currently comfortable purchasing and also if do you've got to get back the cash in order to meet a couple of life responsibilities and requirements for example investing in property, delivering kids to school or retiring.

Like a Beginner lien, you are probably Knowledgeable in regards to the attention you make it in your own savings account, and at the right time of this creating is less than one% annual. This really is just a great example of non risk-reward. In addition, the lender in which you have secured the checking accounts probably provides you FDIC insurance plan (Federal Deposit Insurance Corporation) to the balances. This insurance policies which usedto cover to $100,000.00 per depositor was increased to $250,000.00 for every accounts and can continue to be at the amount before Jan 1, 2014 during which time it truly is counseled to revert into $100,000.00 for each accounts with all the exception of the retirement account that'll always be static in the $250K limit. Possessing this insurance policies is only one of the ways in which you find it possible to restrain hazard. In the event the financial institution fails, the FDIC will pay back you.

In the Contest That You think Inch percentage Interest is decreased, just imagine that which you may possibly be thinking whenever you ascertain the rate of interest will be susceptible to tax once you cover taxes on Uncle Sam regarding the inch percentage you've got, you can wind up getting roughly .66% curiosity rate! In the event you prefer to bring in significantly more focus, then you might think moving a portion of the hard earned money in to a financial institution CD (Certificate of Deposit). The lending institution will give you a very small more awareness in exchange foryou perhaps not bothering the bucks to get a pre determined period of time. Right-now 1-year c d's continue to be simply a sign within 1 percentage along with 5-year c d's are traveling roughly two per cent. If you would like your cash-back before one year old or two 5 years, you can sacrifice quite a few of these focus on a punishment? Nonetheless again, the eye is at the mercy of taxation. By today you need to start to discover that taking on low hazard will me an tiny reward to the time and efforts with a subsequent longer period span ahead of you reach financial flexibility.

Therefore today you Start to Think these really are Fairly poor interest rates and also you begin to check around to get a superior approach to devote your own cash. Whatever you will find is the better part of these services and products that you can spend money on do not arrive with FDIC insurance plan. This means that if the event you'd really like to take a position to them to obtain a superior interest of return, you're have to realize you could potentially withdraw dollars. Just how much income do you really lose? This really is dependent upon what you are purchasing however essentially it has really a fairly grim connection meaning, the more greater pay-off (interest) you hunt, the increased possibility you ought to simply take. . A.k.a. substantial risk-reward. In the event you know to take a position your elevated wages will provide financial independence which far sooner! Here is a truly simple set to clarify that particular connection. Interest speed exhibited is approximate with this particular kind of securities simply because the rates are consistently shifting and it has shown within a annualized basis.

Securities Course Annualized Proportion Reunite

Bonds:

- Treasury 5 year old: 2.65 percentage, 10-year: 3.75 percentage, 30-year: 4.5percentage
- Municipal 3.5percentage to Five percentage
- Corporates 6 per cent to 8 per cent
- Mutual Cash 9 percentage
- Stocks 10 percent to 1-2 percentage
- Annuities:

- Set 4 per cent
- Variable 7 percentage

Commodities/Forex/Options: Incredibly big Interest if performed correctly..20percent and much more is ordinary.

To Obtain some one of the aforementioned mentioned Securities and also many a lot more unmentioned kinds, you are going to need to begin a broker account. While there is not any FDIC insurance policies, you may frequently acquire S.I.P.C. insurance plan (Securities Investor Protection Corporation). It will not shelter you from loss in one's hard earned money whenever the securities had been to fall market price. The stability falls in at which there exists a event of agent home failure or bankruptcy. Protection is approximately $500,000.00 for guaranteed securities and $100,000.00 for your own money. The worthiness of these above mentioned securities can change daily including all the current actions with this market place therefore that it's completely potential that you may get money in the event you decide to dollars from the incorrect minute. If you should be excited to do this threat compared to you will end up paid having a increased interest of return in comparison with about 1% to 2 percent you'd ordinarily receive to some financial savings or C.D. account.

Since you move up the Dimensions of danger along with Reward, which means you are going to be carrying a much increased possibility of shedding the hard earned money!!!

You Understand the danger of searching greater Benefit, usually do not allow it keep you from achieving so. In lifestyle some times you've got to just take some probability to get right ahead of time and reach real monetary liberty. Investing from the stock market can possibly be insecure however, the very optimal/optimally method to soften each the lumps you are going to strike is going to be to diversify between asset classes also to get a lengthy horizon. This isn't hard to reach if you should be saving for retirement however perhaps not very simple in the event that want to get the amount of money earlier such as investing in a house. An principle is the fact that just in the event you are interested in getting the A mount in 3 years or even perhaps not, you really should not be spent in shares as a severe economy correction (go through decline) will probably soon be somewhat tough to overcome 3 years or even not. Additionally bear in mind that during the prior 70 to eighty many years, the stock market has totaled an approximate 10% speed of return.

The Danger and Reward link is well known Well by individuals taking care of Wall-Street even though not therefore nicely with the typical secular individual. In the event you want proof with the particular, maintain a watch out to each the ripoffs you view at the newspapers and on T.V. People eventually become enticed at each one the period including all the current guarantee of top returns. The leading maxim that is"In case it looks too fantastic to be genuine, then it really is".

To outline the subsequent May Be your String of investments out of lowest-risk and lowest salary for a larger chance and increased benefit. The greater danger You Select, the Larger benefit You May anticipate to grab and also the More Quickly You should Be Able to successfully Attain financial liberty:

Financial savings accounts are somewhat less risk-reward than Creditor c.d.'s which is less probable compared to treasury bonds that's less risk-reward than municipal bonds that's less risk-reward than business bonds that's less risk-reward than mutual capital that's less risk-reward than stocks that's less cheaper than inventory decisions.

Bullish Possibilities Buying and Selling Programs

Bullish Alternatives Trading approaches have been Approaches that are satisfactory for once you anticipate the buy price tag of an inherent protection to rise. The most obvious, and most easy, means to profit out of an increasing cost with alternatives would be always to just acquire predictions. But acquiring forecasts decisions isn't of necessity the perfect way to develop a return out of a medium up price motion and this allows no more collateral in the event the underlying security decrease in price tag or never proceed at all.

Applying Plans besides only Purchasing predictions, it's very likely to obtain any notable added benefits. With this particular pagewe look at a couple of the advantages of making use of this options, as well as this pitfalls. In addition, it provides a record of one of the very most often applied kinds.

Why Utilize Currency Alternatives Buying and Selling Programs?

Downsides of Forex Options Dealing Plans

Set of Forex Options Dealing Plans

Purchasing forecasts will be an Approach on its own Suitable, and also there are undoubtedly cases when your exact straightforward acquire of forecasts are going to be described as a viable trade. You will find disadvantages of buying calls too even though. As an example, you experience the threat which the deal which you simply purchase will perish useless and make you no more recurrence at all, meaning that you simply reduce your entire investment decision.

You're going to be more Theme into the Unwanted results of period corrosion, and you're going to probably demand the buy value of their inherent protection to rise pretty considerably in order to get paid almost any profit. That will not automatically signify purchasing phone calls is nearly always a bad notion, as there are potential risks involved with just about any form of investment decision. It is, nonetheless, likely to protect against a couple of the disadvantages by picking out alternative tactics.

Each Forex Currency trading plan comprises its Own different options, and you will have the ability to select an agenda which's almost certainly to work with you to reach whichever it truly is you are looking to get. Byway of example, you can utilize the one that reduces the purchase price tag on purchasing forecasts from additionally composing calls utilizing a high strike. This could also be helpful you reduce the unwanted effect of time rust on your position, some thing that you could do with utilizing an idea that comprised the composing of locations.

Still another Advantage Is Which You Find It Possible to Make credit histories, that give an upfront payment, and as an alternative of debit card spreads which take an upfront selling price. The primary purpose is the fact that using hedging trading procedures, you might enter an area that profits out of a increase in the buy value of this inherent basic safety and restrain additional items that might possibly be considerable for you personally, including the quantity of hazard involved or even the sum of capital demanded.

Cons

Using procedures a Side out of a Easy buy of Call alternatives is maybe not without any negatives although. With nearly any Form of Investment decision, even in the event that you'll love to get extra advantages from your Plan, then you definitely will need to forfeit some thing in exchange. The Specific same is true Authentic for buying and selling

Copy To Clipboard

Edit Spin Copyscape Proofread with

A Spin:

I presume that if You Click on the After record that you are having the impulse to bring in profit stock marketplace. Inside my own experienceI suggest the most lucrative means to make in stock-exchange on the internet is by means of investing. However, to be honest with you, to be wealthy instantly through inventory day trading is equally hopeless, and also unwise to believe that. Like a newcomer, you have must know from flooring upward and will benefit your fiscal flexibility. These recommendations would be the gold rules for those who would like to exchange inside stock market.

As Everyone Probably Knows, Positive Long Term inventory Investment can generate profits along using the number Around 10 percentage per annum if you carry on a certain healthier stock selection. While stock day trading Could Make a strong profit from a trading day trading Time or even briefer. Hence, If You are able to perfect the specialist ability daily trading, it goes to become successful in getting long-term expenditure.

As a Result of This number of business Registered nowadays, stock-exchange offers a number of choices and opportunities. This trend presents better chances for dealers to"refine" and"infusion" the most profitable stock picks. You'll Find broad spread of Stocks that eventually become"hot inventory" each

Week Obey the rapid changing Business weather, such as green, biotech power, online media, mass communication and health care businesses.

The Most Important Variables I Would like to advocate Are the volatility and liquidity of this stock if you're performing day trading. In laymen duration, greater liquidity signifies large dealing frequency whether significant volatility equates to high trading price selection. Neglect those inventory picks with nominal cost movement instead of grabbing eye chunk of dealers.

Another mindset Ought to Be embraced would be to be more Consistent in executing the own trading space. Elect for a solid and good strategy, use essentially the most crucial material and adhere using the fundamental for good. I will urge you could be elastic to control unforeseen circumstances, however don't just change your plan, this will result in the catastrophic effect.

Lastly, even together with the Aid of progress tech stock-trading platform or even hedging strategy, a person has to realize that dealing from the volatile and exceptionally fluctuating stock market entails specified level of danger. You can minimize it but also you aren't able to wholly expel risk taking. My private advice is that do not entails your personal emergency book together with buying and selling. Trade along with your extra cash, that may even let you earn bold but accurate conclusion at critical moment.

Folks Are Continuously Watching out for a Means to flee from the ratrace and also avoid paying hours in the workplace. Most would really like to be able to just work at home and spend more quality time together with their loved ones members as well as friends. However about building the option to initiate a career at home many are scared they'll not get enough money to call home so that any movements away from the rat race will likely be short lived. If you mention to all those people they might eventually become a stock agent and also operate in your home they simply don't believe that you.

Effectively, it really is true. As a result of improvements In modern technologies and the way business is now completed it really is very likely to perform a booming stock broking business from the contentment of of one's own home, just using a notebook as well as a couple of professional pc software. That is thanks, especially, to the currency exchange additionally referred to because the forex marketplace. Using the FX Market you can begin trading foreign currency with relatively little training and expertise, what exactly is it will take just a few hours of your time every day to develop in to a forex dealer while still supplying appreciable rewards (broadly speaking in the six figure range), thus supplying you all the economic freedom you want.

Ahead of you Put away on the Path Growing financial freedom by operating at house you must undertake some fundamental currency trading teaching. The very best approach to accomplish it is to wait for a couple of the numerous inventory broking classes available on the market. In a stock broking course you are going to have the ability to talk to experienced traders that have experienced a lot of success on the money markets. You'll have the capacity to discuss with them the very best way to begin building your own company and figure out in the absolute best means of making trades and the way to cancel your dangers. Additionally you will see that all gains made of the FX transactions are tax free in britain, providing you using a far bigger fiscal incentive to be a stockbroker.

Reaching Risk and Reward

So Exactly What will be possibility and profit? In Lifetime you'll find a great deal of hazards you need to take. Crossing the street is actually a threat. Providentially, a clear bulk of the time, somebody can control that threat. You look both ways before crossing the road. The exact same goes for investment. Getting has inherent hazards but again, an individual could (for some limited scope) restrain the threat. Your fiscal freedom is closely linked with just how much time you choose since it's going to ascertain how much payoff you'll garner from your investments. Everything boils right down to what some people today call"the sleeping factor". How effectively would you like to sleep soundly at night?

Can you enjoy maybe not worry on your Own investments which then will help it become possible that you sleep far better? Or are you really the aggressive kind that wishes to choose for the stars along with your own investments which will force you to forget that a evening or two of sleep? It's mandatory that you choose your tolerance for risk and benefit. By the financial world that's termed an individual's risk tolerance. How do you endure risk? When you start a retirement account or a brokerage account to begin investing, then you will be filling a program which has many queries lots of that will be targeted at detecting your risk tolerance and also a couple will most likely be specific at detecting your own time horizon. In other words, what exactly are you really really comfortable purchasing and if do you've got to get back the cash to be able to meet a few of life's responsibilities and requirements like investing in property, sending kids to school or retiring.

Like a newbie investor, you're most likely Knowledgeable regarding the interest you make it on your savings accounts, and at the right time of this producing is considerably less than 1% yearly. This is really a very good example of non risk-reward. Additionally, the bank in which you've secured the savings accounts likely offers you FDIC insurance plan (Federal Deposit Insurance Corporation) on the accounts. This insurance which usedto pay up to $100,000.00 per depositor was recently increased to $250,000.00 for each account and will stay at the amount before Jan 1, 2014 during which time it's advised to revert into $100,000.00 per accounts with all the exception of a retirement accounts which will remain in the $250K limit. Possessing this insurance policies is simply one of the means in which you find it possible to control hazard. In the event the financial institution fails, the FDIC will reimburse you.

Now in the Contest That You believe Inch percentage Interest is diminished, just imagine what you may possibly think whenever you decide the interest rate will be susceptible to taxation after you pay taxes to Uncle Sam about the 1 percent you earned, you may end up with roughly .66% curiosity rate! If you desire to earn much more focus, then you might look at moving a portion of your hard earned money into a financial institution CD (Certificate of Deposit). The lending institution will provide you a small bit more consideration in trade foryou maybe not bothering the money to get a pre determined time period. At this time 1-year CD's continue to be only a sign over 1 percentage and 5-year c d's are traveling roughly 2 per cent. In the event you want your cash back before one year old or two 5 decades, you may sacrifice quite a few of their attention for a punishment? Yet more, the attention is at the mercy of taxation. By now you need to begin to find that carrying on low risk will me an small reward for your time and efforts having a subsequent longer time interval ahead of you achieve financial independence.

So today you begin To believe that these really are Fairly bad interest rates and you start to check around for a better way to spend your own cash. All you may find is that the bulk of these products that you can invest in do not come with FDIC insurance plan. This implies that if the event you would really like to get to them to obtain a better interest of return, you'll have to see you can potentially withdraw cash. Just how much money can you lose? This is dependent on what you are buying however essentially it has a fairly grim connection significance, the more more pay-off (curiosity) you search, the larger threat you have to take. . A.k.a. huge risk-reward. In the event you learn how to invest successfully your high rewards will bring you financial independence which far sooner! Following is a truly simple list to clarify that connection. Interest rate displayed is approximate for this particular type of securities because the prices are consistently changing and it has shown in an annualized basis.

Securities Class Annualized Proportion Reunite

Bonds:

- Treasury 5 year old: 2.65 percent, 10-year: 3.75 percent, 30 year: 4.5percentage
- Municipal 3.5percentage to 5 percent
- Corporates 6 per cent to 8 per cent
- Mutual Funds 9 percent
- Stocks 10% to 12 percent
- Annuities:
- Set 4 percent
- Variable 7 percent

Commodities/Forex/Options: Incredibly big Interest if performed correctly..20percent and more is common.

To purchase any one of the aforementioned mentioned Securities and also much additional unmentioned kinds, you will have to start a broker account. While there's no FDIC insurance coverage, you may most likely receive S.I.P.C. Insurance (Securities Investor Protection Corporation). It doesn't shelter you against loss of your hard earned money once the securities had been to decrease market price. The stability falls in where there's a event of agent home failure or bankruptcy. Coverage is approximately $500,000.00 for insured securities and $100,000.00 for your own money. The worth of the above mentioned securities will fluctuate each day including all the current actions with this marketplace so that it's completely potential you could eliminate money in the event you opt to dollars from the wrong second. If you are excited to do this threat compared to you will end up paid having a larger interest of return compared with 1% to 2 percent you'd usually receive to some cost savings or C.D. account.

Since you move up the Size of risk and Reward, so you will be carrying a much increased possibility of losing the hard earned money!!!

Now you Know the threat of seeking greater Reward, usually do not allow it prevent you from achieving this. In daily life sometimes you have to consider some probability to get up ahead of time and attain true financial liberty. Investing at the stock exchange can be insecure but the very optimal/optimally method to soften every one of the lumps you may encounter will be to diversify between asset classes also to have a long horizon. That isn't difficult to accomplish if you're saving for retirement however not very simple in the event that want to get the amount of money sooner for example investing in a house. A rule is that just in case you would like the total amount in 3 years or even perhaps not, you must not be invested in stocks because a serious market correction (study decrease) will be rather really hard to conquer 3 years or less. Also try to remember that over the prior 70 to 80 many years, the stock market has shrunk an approximate 10% rate of return.

The Danger and Reward link is understood Well by folks taking care of WallStreet even though not too nicely with the average secular individual. If you require evidence with the, maintain a watch out to every one the frauds that you view in the papers and on T.V. Individuals become enticed at each one of the moment including all of the promise of top yields. The leading maxim that is"When it looks too good to be genuine, then it really is".

To summarizethe Following is your Sequence of investments from lowest-risk and lowest salary to a increased danger and greater reward. The more risk you choose, the greater benefit You Are Able to anticipate to catch and also the sooner you should Have the Ability to Realize financial liberty:

Savings accounts are much less risk-reward than Creditor c.d.'s which is significantly less probable compared to treasury bonds that is less risk-reward than municipal bonds that is significantly less risk-reward than corporate bonds that is significantly less risk-reward than mutual funds that is less risk-reward than stocks that's significantly less cheaper than inventory choices.

Bullish Selections Buying and Selling Programs

Bullish Choices Trading strategies have been Approaches that are acceptable for when you anticipate the purchase price of an inherent stability to grow. The most obvious, and simplest, means to gain out of an increasing cost with alternatives is to just get forecasts. But obtaining forecasts choices isn't necessarily the best way to generate a return from a moderate up price motion and also doing this provides no more collateral if the inherent security decrease in price or not move in any way.

Applying Plans aside from only Purchasing predictions, it is very likely to obtain any notable added benefits. With this pagewe take a look at a couple of the benefits of utilizing this ideas, as well as the advantages. In addition, it provides a listing of the very most frequently used kinds.

Why Utilize Currency Alternatives Trading Options?

Cons of Currency Options Trading Plans

List of Forex Options Dealing Plans

Purchasing forecasts will be an Approach on its Proper, and there are undoubtedly circumstances if a exact straightforward acquire of forecasts will be described as a workable trade. You'll find drawbacks of purchasing calls also nevertheless. As an example, you face the danger which the contract that you purchase will expire useless and make you no more yield at all, which means that you lose your entire investment.

You are always going to be Subject into the Unwanted outcomes of time rust, and you'll probably involve the buy price of the underlying protection to grow pretty somewhat so as to get virtually any gain. This will not automatically signify purchasing phone calls is almost always a bad idea, as there are potential risks involved with any form of expenditure. It is, nevertheless, likely to prevent a couple of those drawbacks by selecting alternative approaches.

Each Forex strategy comprises its Own different attributes, and you will be able to choose an agenda that's probably to work with you to reach whatever it truly is you are likely to get. Byway of instance, you may use the one which reduces the price tag on purchasing calls from additionally writing calls utilizing a high attack. This could also be helpful you reduce the negative effect of time rust in your own position, some thing you can do with utilizing a plan that contained the composing of locations.

Still another Benefit Is that you Have the Ability to Make credit histories, that give an upfront payment, instead of debit spreads that carry an upfront selling price. The primary point is that using bullish trading procedures, you might enter an area that profits from a gain in the buy value of their inherent security and restrain additional activities which could be considerable for you personally, like the amount of risk involved or the amount of funds demanded.

Disadvantages

Using strategies Apart out of a simple purchase of Call choices is perhaps not without drawbacks nevertheless. With virtually any sort of Investment decision, even in the event that you would like to obtain extra benefits from the Strategy, then you have to sacrifice something in exchange. The exact same is True for buying and selling.

The most important benefit of purchasing forecasts is your profits will be infinite, as you are still get the greater the total cost of the inherent security gains. The most significant sacrifice which you create with Forex approaches would be that the prospective profits you'll earn are confined by a certain amount. But considering the fact that lots of choices trades relies on comparatively brief phrase price movements, and also financial instruments usually do not regularly proceed around in cost with large sums; this really is maybe not of necessity an important negative.

Still another Disadvantage could be that the excess complication of attempting to choose the ideal tactic. The thought of buying calls are going to undoubtedly be by it self relatively simple. In the event you were to think that a economic tool increases in price, then then you certainly are in a position to gain out of this increase working with a easy trade. Complicating matters by trying to optimize your possible gains or confine your potential losses definitely requires extra energy and time.

You may an average of pay greater commissions too, due to the fact most ideas expect quite a few of trades to create spreads. But over all you are many more probably be consistently prosperous when buying and selling decisions if you have to know concerning the several trading approaches in order to learn those to make use of and should.

Listing of Forex Options Dealing Plans

The following is really a List of one of the very most usually employed procedures which can be suitable to get a bullish outlook. We have integrated some short advice about every single like the variety of trades are included, whether or even really a debit or credit disperse consists of and perhaps the it really is okay to get a newcomer.

To find more sophisticated details about every plan, such as just how exactly to put it to use, its own benefits, also it's disadvantages, so click the proper url. For aid in selecting a ideal trading system you may desire to use our alternative device to possibilities Trading approaches.

Prolonged Telephone

That really is 1 Ranking plan which involves only inch trade. It's okay for beginners and also can be followed closely through an upfront selling price.

Limited Established

Only one particular Trade is necessary for thisparticular, also it creates an upfront cost. It isn't satisfactory for novices.

Bull Call Spread

This really is a simple Approach okay for beginners. It includes just two transactions to earn a debit disperse.

Bull Put Spread

That really is Straightforward . however, it isn't actually satisfactory for rookies as a result of trading level required. A credit score spread consists of just two transactions.

Bull Ratio Distribute

That can be intricate and desires two transactions; Hence it's perhaps not satisfactory for novices. It Can make a debit distributed or Charge disperse, predicated up on the ratio of options purchased to options written

Brief Bull Ratio Distribute

This relatively intricate trading system isn't perfect for beginners. The two transactions have been included, in addition to a credit score disperse was created.

Bull Butterfly Distribute

You can find two types of bull blossom disperse: calling bull blossom disperse and also the established bull blossom disperse. It's a complicated trading procedure, necessitating three transactions, that creates a banking disperse. It's perhaps not satisfactory for novices.

Bull Condor Pass on

" there are two types of bull condor disperse: that the phone bull condor disperse together side the region bull condor distribute. This tactic requires four transactions also it's perhaps not satisfactory for novices. It generates a debit disperse.

Bull Call Ladder Spread

This really is really a complex trading system necessitating three transactions. It generates a debit disperse plus it isn't satisfactory for novices.

Paying for that the Stock market might be unbelievably difficult to your standard real estate investor and professional investor equally. Inch kind-of stock investing it generally seems to confound virtually every sort of buyer is ShortSale.

Although lots of individuals Know that the notion of brief sale, so many eventually become confounded whenever you start talking informative sale at a bull market place, but that's just what I will talk about within this specific article now because there really are a lot of methods you make significant amount of dollars by means of bull markets utilizing informative sale but this sounds utterly counter clockwise to most common investing and sense strategies!

I'm not planning to bend. Agree into some body that they make short term marketing a foundation of this bull's economy program plus they'll appear in the as you've missed the brain. But, you haven't missed your thoughts at all, you're simply cagey!

The easy Truth About this Item will be through ferocious bull markets we will detect periods of reduction. People now consider this stock exchange gasping for breath right after having a lengthy set. It's those tiny gasps or even downturns that provide chances for sale making and brief a quick buck or two; here and there.

You can find plenty of criteria that you should follow along with along with purchasing brief at a bull market place which could help rescue from receiving clobbered.

Very first sell only intensely capitalized shares that have very low existing curiosity rates. These shares are less very likely to receive hit by a concise squeeze that has a sharp rally which is caused by way of a fantastic offer of short-sellers rushing to pay for their rankings if you can find too many stocks out there there. When a small business doesn't need a significant capitalization and also you want to dash to cover your position, then there may possibly be no inventory readily available to purchase! Bear this in your mind.

Up Coming cover your own errands in the End of the weekend. What is this? Throughout regular bull markets, the favorable news can filter around the weekend that might find the inventory to jump in price tag greatly at first of the subsequent investing week. You usually do not want to wait patiently till afterward advice has turn out within the weekend afterward struggle to pay for your standing over an increasing economy on Monday early morning. It's way better simply to repay before into this weekend when possible.

Up coming usually do not market small-cap term stocks that may have recently established brand new highs or even alltime highs. I know you're likely to become enticed into as it appears plausible a stock that includes increased high may call for a opportunity to refund a little. However, via a bull economy all bets are away and also stocks might keep growing beyond alltime highs without any gasping for breath since it'd been. It's absolutely more advisable to wait definite signs of weak spot after alltime highs ahead of jumping with a succinct place.

Therefore that you have several methods to earn dollars advertising brief by means of a bull-market and masking your self if something else goes wrong once you are attempting to sell short by way of a bull industry. Exactly like expense chances, be sure to acquire your very own homework and also proper investigation before making any investment selections.

Stock-market Approaches for Profitable Purchasing

Mastering just how exactly to hire effective stock-exchange systems might signify that the gap between falling all of your hard-won money or even gaining greater. These tips can enable one for the optimal/optimally investment plans to work with also to prevent those that will still only hurt one.

Know The Business

Prior to you may begin investing, it's essential that you're attentive to the so you can know just how touse true stock-exchange plans. Exploration as far as you possibly can in regards to the present market, these as for instance stocks which interest you - you can find a lot of internet sites and also other benchmark substances that might let you receive yourself a strong grasp with this market place.

Also, coping using a commendable financial adviser or source of creditable financing information is an great stock-exchange strategy touse to really start off to grasp the present market place and exactly what it can do to youpersonally.

Protect Against Infection

Rookies ' are especially at risk of cons and"get rich fast" strategies that are created to entice potential traders to break up with their hard won cash. Unfortunately, the ones who drop for these sneaky stock-exchange plans are not benefiting such a thing; actually, the only real one making the most of these types of sorts of cons would be the natives!

Bottom-line - in case it appears too fantastic to be real, it really will be. Familiarize yourself with all the appropriate expense plans and also comprehension will probably prevent you out of falling to get the ones plans which can be sexy.

Choose a Stockbroker

Implementing an inventory Agent can be actually a huge investment solution to work with, being a commendable broker should be in a position to aid you for making conclusions regarding your own portfolio and lead one to choose the most effective stocks into your personal circumstance. A commendable broker is going to be able to make use of his experience which is going to help you get a superior understanding of this present market place, like developments, stock creation, and also should sell or purchase.

Additionally, a inventory broker can coach you on far better stock investing plans compared to you are likely to detect on your own. A commendable broker will probably be thrilled to assist you along with your portfolio, and also certainly will perform their own best to guide one at the perfect course.

Mastering howto Perform stock market might be described as a frightening prospect, specially for beginner traders. By analyzing on the market; preventing strategies which seem way too fantastic to be legitimate, and also finding a commendable stock broker, it is possible to discover effective stock-exchange plans which is going to help you improve your investment decision into the possibility of profit.

The sum of stock-exchange plans available can make a great offer of firsttime stock dealers eventually become confused concerning exactly what kind to work with while selecting shares. A single's control of those procedures typically requires time plus fantastic amounts of attempt, specially about analyzing and becoming to the nittygritty of investment in. At closing review, the primary differences one of these options lie in just how large investment some body is about to install and at the level of danger you're prepared to become exposed to. Below would be the 3 big tendencies of stock-exchange buying.

One of the most Popular stock-exchange procedures is popularly called the BuyandHold technique. Because its title implies this particular manner is good for longterm investments as the trader commonly purchases the stocks of the certain corporation and keeps them for a exact long period of time. This fashion may likewise be ideal for anyone which are brand new to stock exchange investing or men and women which are risk averse. More times than not, this specific business strategy can be employed by investors to become bluechip shares. If you should be thrilled with making dividends, the buy and also hold mode is actually a wise alternative.

The very best way is another among the absolute most often used stock-market tactics. In the event you are considering by using this particular fashion, then you first have to decide that company or business can be the powerful. For case, in 2008 typically the absolute most well-known businesses to buy will be gold and oil. Once you have settled around the business, the very following thing is always to discover the most recent stocks inside business or small business. The trick to making profits making use of this particular strategy is driving the growth of the business enterprise or perhaps the particular shares. However, this manner can possibly be insecure, specially in the event that you genuinely have no considerable grasp of the firm you picked along with what which can effect the increase and sustainability of this industry. The time of selling and purchasing shares is vital within this type of investment manner.

Ultimately, it's possible to Always elect for cherry-picking or bottoms-up stock-exchange plans. This fashion will not pay attention to the market-place trends or what is transpiring in a particular business. Investors applying this plan generally instruct their sights upon the performance and also costs of all their shares. This type of investment style is also for many women and men with a wonderful bowel feel on which the results are from the industry and people that is able to economically employ small advice to presume about wise alternatives.

One of the exact Interesting goods out of the inventory market, is visiting people market stocks and also participate in market behaviour.

It absolutely had been Evident in your present marketplace reduction. Subsequent to the market was shifting, the crowd has been attempting to sell in any certain price, and inducing the stock market wreck.

In the media, in precisely the same moment, each one the listeners were speaking about selling, advertising, attempting to sell in a uniform chorus.

Since you are able to view in The business actions, the herd suddenly stampeded, not exactly without having warning for a 1 3% economy de-crease in only five weeks until in finish has been reached and then intense volatility abounds.

Imagine should your stock-trading plan ?

Market-place Earning

My experience as an OTC current market delivers me an unique view on these sorts of inventory market stock and trading market crashes.

Envision being truly a expert stock trader, market manufacturer. You have a particular number of finances. If you should be filled up with inventory and usually do not anticipate a stock market crash for example the person we only needed, you are doomed.

If you Have, state $1 billion at stock, to choose a huge quantity, also you also are 80 percent, in A15% market reduction, you shed generally $120,000 at an issue of months. If case you simply experienced to repay your losses, then then you are perhaps not even a happy stock-trading ace.

On the opposite side, within case you're net brief 50 percentage, then you definitely earned $75,000 within simply a handful weeks.

Since you are able to observe being truly a market manufacturer you will either know to expect and benefit from the crowd, or else you will wind up working out boiled liver to get a clerk in a Wall-Street delicatessen simply speaking order. Obtaining carried off with the audience is actually a positive ticket into your deli.

I failed to average 300 per cent a year Pro Fit from my own trading positions in currently being gradual to learn. When I was erroneous, the market-place kicked my bum difficult. Which means you know fast to make the correct reflexes.

here could be your Tricky portion for virtually any stock market trading for market manufacturer - should stock upward, if can be your own foundation, if to ditch, even if can be the best?

That you Do not Need to Become at front of this train and also buy on in the Future. That you really don't want to function as boss the moment the stock market crash seems to discontinue, simply to know industry needs to proceed again.

The Ability To-do so Is Just to Anticipate. You have must be more brief ahead of the reduction, a long time until the growth.

The sole manner you certainly can perform your stock-trading program is to be able to sweep aside each the crowd mentality, each the mini intuition. In the event you find everyone participates, you have must be more trying to liven and proceed fast. In the event you discover everyone attempting to sell a stock market crash, then then you definitely have to start to look for that buy price.

It is That capacity to maintain a obvious mind watching some others as opposed to becoming taken them off with them that leads to profit.

Stock-market Gurus

Consider Warren Buffett obtaining in to Bank of America since it'd become the posterboy into some existing stock market crash. Just awful Information on BOA.

Analyze the wise hedge-fund managers which shorted the home loan corporation until it became clear it was a bubble.

These individuals'd the courage of these heads and also the power to behave in defiance of, in resistance into, the crowd.

Bear in Mind," we don't be at front of this stampeding audience in a stock market crash - overly harmful - yet we do watch for these to create the mistake of over-the-counter the market. If this marketplace shows signals of spinning, we appear to be to buy.

Whenever There Is a Bubble, we look to short.

That is Why the easy plan to become a contrarian works for afew money supervisors.

However, there is more because of this compared to that, a lot more potential for enormous profits. It's mandatory that you trade together with the fad however be expecting, estimate tendencies and market place endings and also appear to be to become in at the perfect price.

Recall it really is lonely. In just one of the greatest predictions, I had my clients primarily in holding and money off acquiring after a market appeared in August

1987. The afternoon after the Oct wreck, " I called them issued an crying purchase proposal as it seemed for me that the panic was exhausted

Itself outside. We had attained the non invasive. A few of them Could collect the courage and also the sum to get, however, people that didn't watched costs which paid down . Buyers had been infrequent along with individuals that were putting out invest in tips were infrequent, however that's become the perfect time for you to buy.

Are you currently starting To recognize that you simply Needs to receive an alternative mind along with also the courage of one's proposal to succeed from the stock market?

Bear Trade

Yet Another Tracking. If You May figure This outside, let me understand. The stocks I have seen come at bear markets. Authentic, you should buy virtually any such thing in a bull-market and also be upward, however also the maximum percent profits in my personal publication are at markets that are poor. Perhaps not horrendous economies, lousy niches. I haven't always identified the reason why.

Stock-market Press

I Would like to Notify You in Regards to the inventory Exchange websites. The commentators are sharp however, also the whole appearance from your press is simply a reflection of crowd believing. In case the market place is shifting, the info presented is positive. Whenever there exists a stock market crash, then no other awesome news can soon look. They seem to focus about the present trend but we all, inside our inventory market trading, even being a problem of inventory market plan, has to count on.

YesIt's a Good Idea to Comprehend exactly what the Present trend is however only since that is the point, first position, at which you will expect.

When There Exists a inventory Market-place crash, then you Expect shift, you are expectant of the rotation point. Whenever there exists a bubble, then then you definitely certainly expect the exploding of this bubble.

That Means You Need To Know the place You're today, However you are always looking in which you are planning the future, then it will be potential to set your self at which you want to become.

There is a Overall trend in Dollar Portfolio and finance professionals to swap the previous a couple of weeks with the market. In case the economy has been upward, they want to buy. In case the economy was down, then they then want to advertise and then proceed fast. Here's the optimal/optimally method to really go bankrupt.

Why Is It That stock traders drop within their investments? For a lot of it's only due to their deficiency of awareness and wisdom. Their trades are based mostly in their own"gut feeling" or even"hunches" and or signs from some other men and women. This could be the incorrect means to perform the inventory market. The things they ought to do would be figuring out the hazard facets incorporated by using their gain aims before leaping into a transaction.

Afterward You'll Find People that educate Themselves also possess the right advice, but nevertheless, they can not restrain their own feelings. Their topic induces their perception to get a non-factor and they consistently continue to stocks at which they presume may flip to receive yourself a profit and conclude in a triumph.

Stock-market plan: Subsequent to the Winner's formula

- Using a plan in Spot and Being/staying persistent.

- firing it by over-trading. Maintain it Uncomplicated.
- Keeping your own losses to 5-15 percentage.
- based Money-management regulations. You Have to Have One setup! Sustaining this emotion in assess Is Probably one of the Most Necessary aspects to some dealer's accomplishment
- Recognizing after you input sector Of course when it is the right time for you to leave.
- And, of course state having the Best Winning way of thinking. This is sometimes tremendously under-rated and should be emphasized additional.

Input Signal and Input strategy:

Realizing when to Input and leave a commerce is Absolutely crucial to get a investor that is effective. Employing these plans can possess a beneficial impact in your own overall results.

- After entering a Market-place: Understanding that the stocks say. This ought to contain technical info and deep research to discover a great idea in your own investment.
- Stop stage: That is actually Actually the point where It's mandatory that you prevent and opt for exactly what you've. Sitting to an inventory which is continuously diminishing could be your guaranteed approach to fall.
- Your Very First Cost goal. You need to to Be attentive to the buy price at which you are going to require your profits in the event the stock exchange investment goes effectively.
- You need to understand Your fundamentals and Let them dictate the very optimal/optimally solution to really go in your own shares. All these fundamentals are put to get grounds and that they

should get adopted to lower your pitfalls each the even though setting you place up to profits.

Seeing a simple Stock market Plan might be rather successful in supplying one of the huge benefits essential to get the stock market. Staying constant and becoming disciplined could be your last secret into your winning system for the success.

For so Several Years, folks Are Wanting to detect the optimal/optimally stock-market tactics. What we need to become careful of about finding out these procedures would be your most truly effective ones which you are able to utilize are the ones which feel suitable for you personally. Since you are whoever will likely be selling and buying the stocks, you have to become sure you truly feel confident and comfortable by yourself personal. For those who are not sure about it advice, then you ought to think about the manner in which you're feeling in case you are generating a go to the stock market that merely will not sense befitting youpersonally. You secure uneasy and shed confidence on your own.

This Could Be Why the Best Possible inventory Market plans are people at which you truly feel cozy generating. You want to fool with the market-place until you know what prices and rates you are comfortable buying and purchasing. You want to pick front how lower it is possible to ensure it is feasible to get a stock value to decline and soon you promote it. Inserting a limitation by yourself is actually a wonderful system to force away losing most your hard earned money. Some people become associated with special stocks due to the fact that they consider they are going to rally. By purchasing each one your stocks as soon as they realize a specific cost can be actually a great way touse.

While You Want To Stay positive in Your Own Stock market plans, just another tactic you want touse will be always to get associated with some stocks. There consistently can develop per day when the stock exchange providing you with one a good offer of dollars will fall and also be worth close to nothing at all. You want to understand beforehand it only is an inventory plus far longer can possibly be ordered. Aren't getting caught up in believing how far money it left you at 1 point you end up dropping most your hard earned money as you saved as much time term.

As anyone in the Stock-exchange business Can permit you to realize the market place modifications every single day, and therefore you have to get ready to generate your own move. As a way to accomplish this, it will also benefit get stock-exchange plans which enable one to find at ease. In case you become uneasy regarding such a thing regarding your stock options, then it possibly was not the perfect option. Exactly the exact same like in whatever you wish to follow along with along with gut intuition. Not only does this really cause you to a lot of money, but however in addition, it might save you away from losing a great deal of money.

Of Each the stock Economy approaches On the current market, the optimal/optimally substitute for you'd certainly be to merely check the inventory exchange. You can find a number of actions you might require to have to really are aware of very well what the true worth with the inventory will be. After are just 3 suggestions to have you all started.

Inch) Blow Off the Fee . When You're Assessing the authentic worthiness of an inventory, subsequently discount the current price. Demonstrably after you choose exactly what it pays and also are considering whether it's a significant acquire or not, then you are going to wish to decide on the buy price tag under consideration. However, at the evaluation position, all of you could might be emphasizing can be your own true price in contrast to the trade worth.

Two) Turn on yesteryear. One Particular telling Variable of just how well an inventory may perform is to appear at it's beyond operation. Take a glance in the prior 2 decades or therefore and observe some significant declines or increases. Make an effort to join using all these highs and highs together with advice regarding the small business. This provides you a fantastic concept of the way a stock reacts to special troubles.

3) Turn into the long run. You Are Going to Want to Research in regards to the organizations whose inventory you're considering acquiring to know exactly what their upcoming plans will be. Together with the advice you'll have collected along how in which the stock reacted to many different stimulus before, you are going to have wonderful notion of the way that it will respond at the long run also.

Should You Obey All these Exact Straightforward inventory Exchange approaches to speed stocks you're going to soon be at a much superior place to create prudent investment selections.

If You'd like cash Now, such like I imply Within a hour, then decide to try what I needed. I am earning far more money now than within my own prior corporation and you also can additionally, navigate the astonishing, authentic narrative, at the hyper link beneath. As soon as I joined I was doubtful about just ten moments earlier I knew what it had been. I used to be smiling from ear to ear and you're going to far too.

A Whole Lot of folks exterior You may discover on The look out for that absolute best stock-market tactics. You'll find quite a lot of schools of thought and it's frequently tough to share with those which are legitimate from their hoop fantasies. Whenever you could be first beginning, the optimal/optimally idea will be to pay attention to the effortless approaches in order to discover since possible proceed.

Inch thought which Usually acts for Beginners would be always to simply opt for a couple stocks intentionally and devote inside them. This can appear counter intuitive, but you can find cases in which it can pay off. The most important thing is the fact that the optimal/optimally approach to understand is by performing. If you take a few of preliminary funds, then commit them in some random stocks and also pay careful attention for the direction that they work you'll purchase a great deal of understanding. In the event you opt to go this course, be certain to perhaps not get down at case you never build an income the bat off. The reason is always to get familiarity, the bucks will appear punctually.

Once You have examined The oceans Marginally, or any time you make the decision to bypass this measure, you may desire to get your research. You can find a lot of different internet sites available that will rate stocks centered on lousy or very good buys. Bear in mind that these are simply remarks, though they truly are often professional remarks. You will need to simply take them to consideration and enable them to guide you towards personally, but don't make it possible for them to be the stock bible. You are going to need to receive your very own additional investigation and tests to better determine exactly what exactly the best deals for you personally're.

The Trick to these Stock trade Strategies for novices is to find familiar accepting risks and comprehending how in which the market place can perform the project.

If You'd like cash Now, such like I imply Within a hour, then decide to try what I needed. I am earning far more money now than within my own prior corporation and you also can additionally, navigate the astonishing, authentic narrative, at the hyper link beneath. As soon as I joined I was doubtful about just ten moments earlier I knew what it had been. I used to be smiling from ear to ear and you're going to far too.

In case you are investing money and Want to Make make money from those investments, so you wish some stock-exchange strategies. You'll locate traders, whose buying and purchasing selections are primarily affected by folks that they understand. They follow exactly what others perform without figuring out what things could be fulfilling to others mightn't do exactly the job in their opinion. The outcome is inescapable from this forex buying and selling and might cause tremendous reduction in the stock market. Around the reverse side, even in the event that you can have an agenda of one's and also you thoroughly abide by this, then there exists a far better possibility you may succeed later on and make lucrative stock-exchange investments.

Produce An agenda - The very Very First and foremost Matter Is always to attract stock-exchange plans by yourself. For this you wish to receive yourself a exact clear understanding of those readily available stock sorts and assorted processes of accomplishing stockmarket . Byway of example, you'll find many different inventory sorts, for example big cap, mid capstocks, small cap stocks, small cap stocks, sector stocks, growth shares, volatility shares etc..

These have Their Specific features Rather than most the inventory type s are okay for a certain investor. Afterward you'll see trading types, so you have the capacity to to do forex trading, then which means you may put money into currency section, and additionally you can play daily buying and selling or else you find it possible to take a position in long-term. Once you have obtained comprehensive grasp of the benefits and pitfalls of each of these buying and selling sorts and in addition possess a crystalclear grasp of this hazard associated with each sort of trading, then subsequently take notes on your skill as well as your openness to look at such threats. You then are ready to detect the most suitable way for your own stock market investments.

Consistently create a long term strategy -. Until investing instock market, it really is always better than find yourself a longterm stock-exchange tactic. It will not of necessity signify that you should buy a inventory and await weeks as well as weeks. Quite a longterm plan is to find yourself a pre-defined entry and exit details to get a particular stock and abide by along without fail. This may guarantee you might profit on your own trading.

Adhere to this fundamentals - Even Though forming Your inventory market strategies, stick to the basics with the market. Follow positive results of this technical investigation and basic search and choose conclusions based with this particular. Do not be confused together with most of the current sudden tendency shift around the present market rather than give in driving a car. After you have accomplished your analysis nicely and still have a pragmatic strategy to follow abide by it and you're going to benefit from the log price. To truly have the best way for the inventory investments you might additionally check with a knowledgeable broker or currency markets analyst.

Stock marketplace Investment tips really are a dime a dozen. And as stock exchange program is readily on the list of exact diverse and common offerings that you will encounter. Thus many stock-exchange plans exist considering that every single investor buys stock shares having an agenda that's appropriate to those because somebody. Investment hints really are simply some body telling the others what stock stocks appear to do the job with their own stock-exchange plan. There isn't every means to detect a more stock-exchange plan compared to simply to come across your own personal.

Each so called'ace' will Supply one Investment hints, however do the exact tricks work a lot more usually than they don't really? Perhaps not, also this is a result of how the stock-exchange aims of those'gurus' do not comprise one of the most indispensable section: period.

If It comes in Stock trade Approaches, timing is simply being aware of when to purchase when to promote receive the most economically lookup final results. If your focusing on just how exactly to devote stocks, subsequently understand that time is obviously probably the most necessary portion. Exactly why? Considering every stock-exchange plan revolves across the elderly'purchase low sell large' ideology.

In Reality, the Majority Of the typical stock market Plans aren't anything greater than the usual method to see when the minimum price tag along with the huge selling price come about (reverse should shorting). Once you are ready to begin with to buy stock shares once you think that enough timing is correct, since it reaches a point it'll trickle out from, then you desire on both hands portion of this stock-exchange mystery.

It's Mandatory That you know to perform buy when it is At ease for you personally you never kindly purchase stock shares because somebody else informs anyone to achieve that. Blind opinions are inherently insecure since they truly are man envisioned therefore might be far more inclined to inaccuracy. Likelihood of mistake is the reason you want to maybe not let investment decision tips guide your own financing. T-AKE investment tips for quite a proposition which might be properly used being a consequence of funnel further due-diligence.

Once You Work out the Direction You like To get the lows, then you simply should find out the way to sell. The only investing hint I Had back, is to develop into covetous. Whilst I possess the belief drift off, I truly do. Period of Time. What if I miss extra benefits? A benefit is just a reward. I had much rather have a far greater profit when compared to weight reduction, each day.

Given Possible Identify in case you Feel it is best to get, and also you're ready to spot whether it really is you're Comfortable carrying an gain or loss, then congratulation, you have your own personal Personal inventory market arrange for investment. Stay Glued into this Specific plan And accommodate as possible proceed. That is exactly what all of Expert dealers perform when they Spit out purchasing hints. In case some individual Experienced a reliable or repeatable Process That obtained a steady ROI, then everyone could make use of it. No machine in This Way Exists because every person is special and demands their own tailor-made Stock exchange programs.

Bull Market Strategies for Investors

Investors Can use a Number of Procedures To put money into the stock market. To get started with, they need to take a look at marketplace developments, learn more in the market place at which in fact the firms they truly are contemplating work, and purchase stocks at a suitable minute.

Commonly, Fantastic Businesses declare their Profits, or so their reputation around the present market, at distinct periods of this season. The charges of these stocks often rise earlier such invoices are manufactured. So, traders need to be watching for these phases, and never purchase stocks only at that time. In other words, it really is crucial wait the most useful'Marketplace Interval' for buying and selling in shares. Some basic Stock-exchange strategies for traders will be listed under: -

Produce a Well Orchestrated Expenditure portfolio Which fulfills a particular level of risk tolerance.

Maintain studying and peeling the Investment portfolio to remain educated about marketplace tendencies.

The specialized Assessment of shares assists in Gaining greater comprehension in regards to a firm: its own profits, its economy capitalization, and also its own upcoming growth potential customers. Equally important is to be able to grasp and utilize the qualitative steps of this stock market.

Ever since investing from Your inventory market is. Intricate, in experienced dealers must look to get support out of financial advisors and inventory analysts before committing their own cash.

The slogan Getting"Get Low and Economy Substantial", always buy stocks when their premiums are somewhat not low, and also offer them as so on when the price goes upward.

Invest sensibly. An sharp comprehension of This market, using a wonderful grasp of the company that you simply plan to invest in, assists in generating improved investment decisions. Investors ought to extensively find out more about industry at which in fact the picked corporation will work.

Long term eyesight and prep will be Crucial. Investors ought to appraise their funding edge, and set their allowance limits, before buying an organization. This means, knowing when to continue into the shares, also if to discontinue.

It is normally Suggested to devise and Apply a depart plan attentively. Investors can create their death whenever they will have gained amazing returns over a certain time.

The returns gained By promoting the shares Of a company could possibly be reinvested in some additional, promising larger profits.

Investors must likewise set their tolerance Limitation to your entire sum of decrease they truly are ready to endure whether the business remains still down. They can leave whether their reductions plan or cross their given limit. This process of limiting the number of decrease a invest or may withstand is usually named"Cease loss-limit".

Still another strategy Investors may trace Is to'Buy and alter Frequently'. Researching the market suggests that every business has any restriction regarding the estimated benefits of these shares. Investors can hence go out of an inventory whenever they will have reached maximum yields from shares so. It truly is vital to put money into a lot of organizations to withstand the declines of some.

The Intention of Any Investment Decision would be to maximize Yields while lowering dangers. Diversification may aid in optimizing yields from investments in stocks and bonds from tackling threats improved. Investors also will need to distribute their trades around many types as an example foreign securities and mutual resources to be about the flip side, and also at the procedure enjoy yields that are fantastic.

The approaches to Handle the realities of Existence and to face realities of this stock-exchange are equally. Problems cannot be averted in either different locations. But choices are all readily available. You change your own apparel predicated around the climatic problems. You only takeout woolens during winter months also texture comfy with a cotton tshirt throughout the summer. Much like does work with this particular Exchange local climate. Whenever you imagine its own mood is not satisfactory on your own portfolio, then and then you definitely have to preserve a exact low profile. Wait patiently and await the right prospect. You are to the defensive now.

Defensive Inventory Promoting approach means to Take lesser risks or not any threats. Avoid these unstable stocks and also be more happy with common advantages. Individuals who own the bookings of wealth by preceding earnings wont be fearful to accept atomic places through the aggressive states available on the market. To this specific's offense could be the optimal/optimally kind protection.

Subsequent to the Market-place become inconsistent, The very top of those analysts and analysts fail, which is advisable for your buyer to eventually become more watchful. Say short-term good bye in to the market and devote the bucks for smaller durations in financial institution deposits and remain tension-free. Or invest in bluechips. They may be pricey stocks. The circumstance is really, maybe not with reasons, because of this's your investment that is secure. The expenses will probably be counter to a level, with the sizeable yields inside the type of wages.

What only way by Plan Is-also, its own Span will be to get a temporary time period. It truly is concerning the requirements becoming in a particular minute. In the event you believe the share industry just is not the perfect locale for one to find yourself a quite long time, then esteem your appraisal and also attract a wonderful chunk of investment decision from this portfolio and then go for more powerful investment decisions including treasury bonds of USA. The returns are rather very low, however guaranteed. You've the delight of donating to your societal origin.

These kinds of bonds are floated using a couple noble social objects in outlook.

To Receive a brand new entrant in conversation Assets, the defensive plan is not only desired, however it truly is absolutely vital You're a master in concepts related to all the share industry, you're Chartered Accountant, Cost Accountant or Certified Fiscal Analyst. Nevertheless, that the tempest in your trade, since it stalks ferociously, stinks out everything. Some people who possess high operational practical experience shake and collapse. The optimal/optimally policy is to simply take moderate challenges, whenever you produce a decent total by buying and selling . You may profit greater returns, however your revenue in know-how are affluent plus so they'll stand you in very good stead for prospective obligations.

Defensive Inventory Promoting plan may Likewise function as the lasting coverage of one's investment decision. Your portfolio should remain diversified, as you can find a number of expense opportunitiescatering to suit your own wants for assorted stages of someone's own life. Your broker will give you information on those investment decisions. Dividend reinvestment application is only one single such stable topic of investment decision. The large part of the treasury bonds are also nice. Since they truly are exempt in the state and local taxation, the web yield from the 3-5 per cent tax bracket, proves to somewhere around to 3-5 per cent.

Lots of these Organizations cover really Substantial dividends. Even throughout the hardest slide within the talk industry, their premiums are not much influenced.

Like a wise shopper, It's Necessary for You to watch The warning signs and demand prompt surgical actions. When explosive countries predominate out of your trade, a day's delay will probably cause you to more significantly. To make an optimist is excellent, but tend not to accept assurance about the bounds of carelessness. Cast a side the imaginings something dramatic will probably come about and additionally the share costs will probably appear. Walking up hill is always tricky, which retains fantastic also towards the scenarios connected to all the trade.

The first Point to Understand about inventory market Aims is there are no actual collection plans that are sure to use for all those. The socalled market professionals really are a dime a dozen plus certainly will try to persuade one for a low-cost their primary options are guaranteed to show you in millionaire. This isn't actually authentic, also in the event you own some amount of shared feeling, you knew that. The easy facts are any strategies, information or advice anybody delivers you about the inventory market, actually from skilled dealers, is simply a re telling of the plans which have looked to work to these. And you're going to only need to get what will work for you personally.

The Principal Point to Be Careful of when you place Outside to locate your stock-exchange strategies is the fact that point has become easily the most necessary portion. From the inventory market, timing entails comprehending when could be the perfect period for selling or purchasing inventory therefore that you stand to find the utmost profit. The refined areas of time demand being the capacity to really feel every time a stock has attained its lowest or lowest value ahead of turning and moving in yet another way. Simply keep in your mind the oldest market plan of period, acquire sell and low highquality.

Still another Substantial Point to Stay in Your Mind About stock market strategies is you ought to create your decisions to buy and market that are best for you personally, and also only you personally. Don't allow anyone else let you know and things to get. Purchasing inventory kindly because some body else ensured it had been the most perfect action to do is the initial worst and first novice inventory buying and selling mistake. Purchase first and only invest in and offer stocks you've explored and are so of the opinion will get the job done for you personally.

Very last, remember Simply to threat so Far as you May endure to reduce, as if you have got profit the markets, even it truly is in peril, albeit the threat may possibly be comparatively tiny. Starting studying and small while you proceed is likely the wisest method at all. Exactly enjoy every investment investing, make sure to run your inventory plans out of the fiscal advisor or stockbroker prior to making any huge decisions. Whenever these specialists won't need each one the replies, ideally they will possess the critical experience including all of the pros and cons of the currency markets to tip out awful thoughts prior to you have a chance to behave on them.

Looking for an Excellent investment for Generate? People now invest chiefly in order that they really can get yourself a great return as a result right now. With all the existing financial illness anguish more with each and every passing day, individuals are wanting to know who will be the perfect destination for a invest in. As stated by a couple investors who the stock market still essentially the very coveted site.

You Need to Be Thinking about precisely what exactly Are we stating since the niches have been highly influenced. We concur totally that the markets continue to be lasting but in the event that you should be looking to get a opportunity for a millionaire immediately afterward the stock-exchange can be the safest bet.

It's not We could assure you a Million dollars out of the stock exchange immediately however you'll find special items that might assist or guide you towards victory at the stock market. Simply abide by this processes provided under and forth executing such being fully a millionaire wouldn't may actually be always a difficult endeavor.

- Take A Proper Plan In-place Prior to Starting Dealing:

Most Women and Men suffer tremendous declines Simply because they simply do not possess a wonderful enough prepare rather than Figure out which type of shares can possibly be helpful for you personally and can reap some amazing historical outcomes. Create proper observe of these dangers that you can decide on after which chalk out on an plan, remember a threat will yield tens of thousands of thousands of tens of thousands of bucks in case it truly is well-calculated or you also might make you reduce tens of thousands of tens of thousands of bucks.

- Strive to Adhere To some Longterm Plan:

Most Women and Men Think Inventory market is The perfect locale for shortterm investment however do you really realize that a clear vast majority of the most significant benefits that are created out of the stockmarket encounter from longterm financial commitment. Give it a go and create countless!

- Practice Every One of those Rules:

Accomplishment in Practically Any Subject is got from Adhering to the fundamental regulations. So could be true with stock-exchange, abide by the rules and get top returns!

There are Several Different tricks too, however be Sure you simply observe the fundamentals mentioned previously while they are able to flip you in millionaire immediately!

If You'd like cash Now, such like I imply Within a hour, then decide to try what I needed. I am earning far more money now than within my own prior corporation and you also can additionally, navigate the astonishing, authentic narrative, at the hyper link beneath. As soon as I joined I was doubtful about just ten moments earlier I knew what it had been. I used to be smiling from ear to ear and you're going to far too.

Envision doubling your money weekly Little if any threat! To locate an established listing of million-dollar Firms offering their product in 75 percentage commission to youpersonally. Follow the hyper link under to comprehend the method that you'll begin compounding your capital onto your own very first Million bucks from the very simple company money application.

"Dollars Earning Money," I would Love to Listen to folks state by that I climbed up. In the event that you want to acquire money out of the stock market, then it is crucial never to pay for an excessive amount of attention on every day published daily. Read attentively in the event the business is certainly going down or up, and from just how far, however skip the offthecuff reasoning. Write-down a few notes of those news activities which may affect the monetary natural environment - that an increase or decrease in taxation will own effect on earnings gains, a copper-industry strike in USA that can mean bigger expenses and much more business to Canadian copper manufacturing companies. Watch brand new reports about organizations with stocks listed on the stock markets, especially the businesses whose stock you've obtained or are contemplating paying for. But do not allow your view with this business outlook vary in a reaction to this opinions released daily. In the event you are doing, subsequently yo will perhaps not even hold your opinion to behave about this, and you're going to become an anxious mess out of this agreement.

Making Your personal Perspective with This Outlook for that present economy, and staying with this before states definitely reveal you are erroneous, is just one of both major approaches of playing with the activity it self dependent method. Successful stock-exchange traders do not hunt with this crowd. They stalk their prizes from isolation that is lonely, thereby thinking the consensus perspective into this near future is broadly speaking erroneous - an notion together with substantially evidence to encourage it. That really is so stark opinion is not really as absurd because it sounds whenever you experience it. Stock charges grow whenever you will find more folks ready in buying compared to attempting to sell. It must not be surprising, even there, which the greater part of traders are bullish until industry boils along with before a falling market turns out, you may scarcely locate a Realtor that is foreign.

The following Strategy will be to discount that the Hullabaloo in excess of what exactly the business will probably perform. Many flourishing stock exchange traders do this. Academic proof signifies there is no connection between just what the market did yesterday and also that which precisely it's likely to execute today, a few weeks or even monthly - that the socalled randomwalk idea. There is additionally a good deal of historic evidence which suggests it really is useless to try to predict the method by which a stock market will answer economic advancement from the short-term. Being an case, it had been believed nearly a pure occurrence that traders will react to enthusiasm to market which's expanding quicker than predicted. But sporadically while in the last year or two, traders have not always bombarded advice about faster-than-expected enlargement with zeal. So, even in the event you'd accurately called any particular piece of economical fantastic news, then you then would not have done well from the stock market by making a shortterm investment depending on your prediction.

Fiscal Bull market

Monetary markets refer widely to some Market at which the investing of securities transpires, as an instance, inventory market, bond exchange, foreign exchange, and derivatives market place, and many others. Monetary markets are quite valuable for the smooth operation of markets.

Understanding the Monetary Markets

Monetary markets fit a Crucial Function In easing the smooth operation of markets by leveraging capital and producing money for organizations and internet marketers. The markets ensure it is simple for buyers and sellers to swap their fiscal holdings. Monetary markets generate securities services and products which extend a yield for those who've excess finances (Investors/lenders) and also make such capital offered to folks who need additional cash (debtors).

The Stock-exchange is just Inch kind of Financial sector. Monetary markets are produced by buying and selling different sorts of fiscal instruments like shares, currencies, bonds, and derivatives. Monetary markets count seriously on informational Transparency to guarantee that the markets establish prices that are appropriate and efficient. The current market prices of securities may not be due to this Intrinsic significance as a result of financial forces such as taxes.

Some fiscal markets really are modest little Motion, and numerous more, like the New York Stock Exchange (NYSE), trade trillions of bucks of securities daily. The shares (stock) marketplace can be really a financial Market which enables traders to get and promote shares of publicly traded organizations. Even the most important stock-exchange is really where fresh topics of stocks, called First public offerings (IPOs), are available. Any next investing of shares whined from the market, in which investors purchase and sell stocks that they have.

Sorts of Monetary Markets

Over the Counter Markets

An Overthecounter (OTC) marketplace is really a Decentralized market --significance it will not possess physiological spots, also trading was conducted --at which exchange traders exchange stocks directly among 2 parties without a broker. An OTC economy oversees the market of publicly traded stocks that are not listed to the NYSE, Nasdaq, or even the American Stock Exchange. Broadly speaking, organizations that exchange on OTC markets are somewhat marginally smaller when compared with those ones which exchange on markets that are main, as OTC markets require regulation and cost significantly less to make use of.

Bond Trade

A bail is really a Safety at which a investor loans Income to have yourself a predetermined time in a predetermined interest rate. You also may possibly look at a bail as a arrangement involving your lender and debtor that includes the specifics of this loan together having a unique duties. Bonds are issued by businesses along with by municipalities, countries, and autonomous governments to invest in projects and operations. The bail marketplace sells securities such as statements and notes issued by america Treasury," as an example. The bond industry has been also called the charge, as well as fixedincome business.

Funds Trade

On Average, the Forex market exchange in. Goods with highly liquid shortterm maturities (much less than one calendar year) and are distinguished with a top degree of stability and also a relatively low return .) At the wholesale amount, the money markets require large-volume trades between institutions and traders. At the retail amount, they also include income market mutual capital ordered by investors and money accounts started by creditor customers. Individuals can also invest in the bucks markets by paying for short-term certificates of deposit (CDs), civic notes, as well as U.S. Treasury invoices, one of other scenarios.

Derivatives Overall Economy

A derivative is a Deal involving in Least 2 celebrations whose values is currently predicated in a undercover inherent fiscal advantage (for example, being a basic safety) or set of tools (for example, an indicator). Payments are secondary securities whose value will be solely based in the worth of their primary security they've been connected. In and of it self which the derivative remains futile. As an alternative of investing in stocks directly, a derivatives market place trades in shares and selections trades, together side other advanced financial goods, that derive their value from underlying tools like bonds, commodities, currencies, currency interest rates, current market indexes, stocks and shares.

Forex Trading Overall Economy

The Money (forex) marketplace is Your market where players could buy, market, sell, and speculate online currencies. Hence, the money exchange has become easily the most liquid market place in the whole environment, as currency has become easily the most fluid of funds. The currency exchange oversees $5 trillion in every day transactions, which is greater compared to fraud and equity markets united. Similar to most of the OTC markets, the currency market might be is composed of the global community of agents and servers from all around the entire world. Even the currency market includes banks, banks, business organizations, central banks, banks, investment management companies, hedge funds, and retail currency agents and agents.

A fiscal marketplace is Merely as much Mechanism as it truly is really a spot, potentially an electronic or even a physical 1, at which buyers and sellers as well as middlemen meet to run trades in securities, securities and alternative exchangeable matters of values. Hence stocks, bond, gold and silver coins, crude oil and agricultural services and products might function as area of trade from monetary markets.

The financial Stock market is the Technical location for several matters related to shares of stocks issued by the people exchanged firms outlined in the stock exchange. The apparatus exchanged is your stocks or inventory whereas the stock exchange could be your mechanics or place at which the trades are all performed. The single section of sellers buyers, and traders can be now found.

The Stock-exchange is a Part of the entire Capital markets at the essential function will be, naturally, to boost financing. That can be contrasted with most of the current derivatives market place where in fact the transfer of threat would be your own main goal along with all the currency markets at which global transaction is its essence.

The financial Stock-exchange raises Capital for all many organizations throughout the issuance of shares. Fundamentally, business matters talk of stocks in to the shareholders also contains really paid for all these stocks, and therefore, raising their fiscal capital. Byway of example, in the event the company issues 1000 shares of stock coming in at $100 worth, then then it might boost $100,000 in cold money.

The price each Go over is put in the amount Worth (price tag cited around the inventory certification) or perhaps the industry price (price tag at which the stock exchange is appreciated in the completely free market predicated over a variety of factors). It needs to be noted that it really is that the industry significance where stocks of stocks are acquired and sold to the stock markets. The degree value may be properly used for legal purposes like in Money supply.

Otherwise, you May Discover That The financial inventory Exchange includes 2 pieces - secondary and chief niches. As their titles imply the primary marketplace could be where newly-issued shares of shares are introduced into the system whether the secondary market-place allow both traders and investors to buy and offer securities.

Being Aware of the Groups of the inventory Exchange is not all there's for it. You Want Going to on the Publications and navigate the entire world Wide net, request the experts and discover the exact advice so you are able to Make probably the maximum Of the profit opportunities and chances inside the financial Stock market. Start now And possibly to morrow You Are able to start making your primary Stock profits.

www.ingramcontent.com/pod-product-compliance
Lightning Source LLC
Chambersburg PA
CBHW050001230526
45465CB00003BB/1205